"*The Warrior's Dilemma* does an outstanding job of addressing the many challenges that military veterans face when transitioning from military to civilian life. Dylan Bender's analysis of military transition is thorough and accurate due to his years of military experience and as a licensed combat readjustment counselor. The single greatest strength of the text is that it not only identifies the many challenges that veterans encounter during transition, but also provides strategies to mitigate and overcome them. I recommend that this text is provided for all veterans while attending their military transition seminar so that transitioning veterans have the proper tools for themselves and families as they create a new identity and thrive within their new civilian life.

Wallace "Mike" Mains, Sergeant Major USMC Retired
Doctoral Candidate, Pepperdine University

"*The Warrior's Dilemma* offers a unique approach to understanding and addressing the challenges faced by veterans and successful transition into civilian life. And it's pages Dylan takes us through the process of becoming a member of our armed forces and the psychological effect on one's personal identity that comes with it. Through this analysis of why this transition changes establishes a foundational shift in the veteran persona we getting clarity on the challenges in returning to the norm of private life as a citizen following service. Whether you're a veteran yourself or you're trying to understand a close loved one to you. *The Warrior's Dilemma* serves as a compass towards understanding and acceptance of the realities faced by another generation of Warfighter. As a personal friend of Dylan I can attest to the goodness of his approach as he has brought into my life. Through his one to one therapy using his methodology of this book I have finally found peace which has alluded me during my own experience of and relating to war fighting and its transition. It's my honor to be able to get back to his efforts through endorsement of his book to all who will listen those of us who have served, and those who have has supported us deserve peace in our next chapter of life. Within the chapters of the warrior deliver you will find the root cause of the tools towards understanding the veteran identity, and their application, the routes towards purple for action outside of it."

Brian Jacklin, USMC MARSOC retired

"If you are a veteran transitioning to civilian life, a family member or spouse supporting a loved one who served, or a professional assisting veterans with the multifaceted and complex issues commonly experienced by the military community after discharge this book is for you. As a veteran and veterans counselor working in higher education for over a decade, *The Warrior's Dilemma* is a power tool that identifies the difficulties veterans experience after service, explains the root causes of these challenges and offers solutions that work. This is an essential tool for all who served and/or work with those that have. "

Kolin Williams, Army Veterans Councellor

"If you are a veteran or soon to be, read "*The Warrior's Dilemma*"! After 34 years of uniformed service and 32 years of marriage the why behind so much is finally revealed. It feels like Bender was in my drop pouch my entire career. It's masterfully written for the target audience (Warriors) from our perspective, insight, and culture! You are not broken you are exceptional and your skills when adapted offer all the elements needed for transition success. Beyond insight, Bender provides the tools for your next mission, Purpose, and Vision. You and the ones you love have earned and deserve this!"

Chris Ruediger, U.S. Navy EOD Senior Chief (ret) Police Officer/ SRT member (ret)

Who is this guy?

—————————— ★ ★ ★ ——————————

Dylan Bender is currently a combat readjustment therapist with the Veterans Health Administration Vet Centers program. He works with active-duty and veterans transitioning back into the civilian life after a combat deployment(s). He has been working in this area for 15 years and has over 25,000 clinical hours in working with veterans and their families readjusting after service in the military. Dylan also served in the Marine Corps for 8 years as an infantry and reconnaissance Marine. He got out of the Marines in 2004 to pursue his education in clinical psychology. Dylan did his graduate work at Azusa Pacific's Graduate School of Psychology. He received an M.A. in clinical psychology, with emphasis in Marriage and Family Therapy. He is also married (20 years) and has three children, all of whom add great meaning to his life. Dylan is currently involved with developing and implementing programs that are addressing transitioning out of the military, marriage failure rate, suicide epidemic among the military, and military performance psychology.

——————————— DISCLOSURE ———————————

Acknowledgments

★ ★ ★

I first have to say that I never had the ambition to take on the endeavor to write a book. My thought was that there're already so many books out there that have good content and are addressing the needed issues. After the influence of the many people that follow I began to realize that I needed to write a book about an ongoing issue that is creating so much difficulty for so many warrior's and is nothing address well.

The list of those who believed and invested in me is innumerable but there are a key few that their impact was prompting to initiation of this process. First, I thank all the warriors who have entrusted me with their experiences. Truly they deserve acknowledgment for carrying the burden of the military experience, and I seek to honor their experiences.

Next, I thank you Randy for making the investment of time and money to start this journey. Your mentorship and wise advice have been invaluable to me.

Steve and Susie Perry. I cannot go without saying Steve and Susie Perry with the Sacred Harvest Foundation that invested in me to make it impact for the military. Truly, I would not have been able to start the process and help fellow warriors if it wasn't for their support. I am tremendously grateful for their generous and visionary hearts.

I am so grateful to my wonderful bride and children who gave up the time with me so that I could piece together this book. I am so grateful for my loving wife who believes in me and supports me with her love and compassion. Finally the one who is ignited my heart to make a greater impact with my life. My King and my Captain, my Savior Jesus Christ. I truly could not produce any fruit outside of Him

THE
WARRIOR'S
DILEMMA

★ ★ ★

D. A. BENDER

The Warrior Dilemma

Your Guide for a Successful Transition to a Satisfying Civilian Life

Dylan Bender

Copyright © 2022 by Dylan Bender

ISBN 979-8-35091-079-7

Contents

———— ★ ★ ★ ————

★ ★ ★

Stuck Between Worlds

You don't have to look far to find whole shelves of books on the military experience, or on getting out of the military and returning to civilian life. Some of these books try to answer the question, "Why is it so hard for many warriors to make the transition from a military culture to civilian life?"

Many such books, however, miss a key issue—and missing it creates tremendous problems for warriors. In *The Warrior's Dilemma* I want to unpack that issue and show you how dealing with it more effectively can make all the difference. As one Marine stated:

> I had no idea of the actual impact, the gravity of the impact, that getting out would have on me. After I got out, three or four couples that have been out two or three years tried to tell me, "It may take a year, year and a half, before you're right." And they knew, all right. Well, why didn't y'all tell me beforehand, guys?
>
> But what that did tell me is that at least 90 percent, 95 percent, of warriors who get out go through this and no one talks about it. But every single one of them said it happened to them.

This book will help you along this difficult path. I want you to be informed and to help you understand how to make your way through it. Too many of our brothers and sisters simply can't navigate this difficult terrain on their own. We are going to talk about it and give you an edge in going through this.

So, What's the Key Issue?

The key is *not* about getting a great new job; the issue goes far deeper than that.

Nor is the key issue a pathology of some kind, whether PTSD or something else.

In fact, the most common reason for this tough transition grows out of the very things that made us the best war fighters in the world. Without properly addressing these issues, warriors can find themselves confused, frustrated, angry, hopeless, depressed, and even suicidal.

The key is about finding and embracing your core, unchanging identity, which depends on a pair of complementary issues. Warriors must address both issues to successfully transition from a military culture to a civilian culture.

> The key is about finding and embracing your core, unchanging identity.

First, they must understand that the nature of the difficulties they face are rooted in circumstances far more profound than simply finding a new career or getting diagnosed with some pathology/disorder.

And second, they must apply their new understanding in real-world ways that will equip them to successfully make the transition.

I unpack both issues in this book.

Why Should You Listen to Me?

For more than a decade I have worked with warriors as they leave the military, or with other men and women who once served in the military but who continue to struggle with transitioning to civilian life. I write this book for them, so that their experiences of the struggle will help future warriors. I hope that reading about their struggles will help you to overcome your own challenges and to help you understand and navigate the complexity of the task before you. I do not write representing any organization, but am evaluating my personal experiences, the experiences of others who have gone before me, and many who have come after me.

My background, I work day in and day out as a readjustment therapist, I hold an MA in clinical psychology, and am a licensed Marriage and Family therapist. As a former reconnaissance Marine, I have noticed troubling patterns taking place in my area of responsibility. After leaving the Marines, I have logged more than 20,000 direct clinical hours working with combat veterans and their families in the areas of transition and trauma. I can therefore say with confidence that:

- Most transition issues are *not* driven by pathology (some type of disfunction).
- A sizable majority of the veterans I work with have experienced most of the issues addressed in *The Warrior's Dilemma.*

While I do not claim to be an infallible authority on this topic, I do provide *the perspective of a warrior working clinically in this field* to help thousands of veterans make the transition more successfully. Please note, you are not reading just my words; you are reading the words of thousands of warriors who have struggled deeply. Out of their own anonymity they are not quoted directly, unless it is specified.

I have worked with service members from each branch of our armed forces. I also have been privileged to work with several generations of veterans, from World War II to the conflict in Afghanistan. Although their training and conditioning methods differed in various ways, a few core principles lie behind the foundation of how *all* our military services work. We will discuss these principles to highlight the problems that countless transitioning military personnel encounter and to point the way to a more successful life as a civilian.

Many Tribes, One Culture

As you read what's ahead, keep in mind that "warrior culture" can take many forms. Native American culture, for example, boasts many tribes, each of which has developed its own unique culture for training warriors. Still, each tribe remains part of the Native American warrior culture.

And so it is with the different "tribes" of the U.S. military. Within this larger warrior culture, different tribes—Army, Navy, Air Force, Marines— use various methods and techniques to cultivate and prepare their own warriors. Some tribes use more extreme methods and conditioning than others. As a former Marine, many of my stories and reflections come out of the

Marine culture; but I have worked with all military tribes. Their stories, too, will echo throughout this book.

To highlight certain lessons, I also have used examples from my own personal transition. In addition, I have conducted in-depth interviews with many warriors from the four largest branches of the U.S. military to get their stories and insights, which they have graciously given me permission to use. Finally, I have presented the information in this book to members of every military branch and consistently hear that it resonates with their own experience.

> I have but a single goal: to suggest how we might be more intentional about preparing our warriors to transition back into civilian life, while continuing to encourage them to hold onto the unique power of the warrior identity.

Throughout *The Warrior's Dilemma* I describe existing forms of conditioning in the military, but I do not recommend any changes to those conditioning methods. The U.S. military has refined the making of warriors to an art and a science, and I have no desire to compromise our nation's mission effectiveness. Rather, I have but a single goal: to suggest how we might be more intentional about preparing our warriors to transition back into civilian life while continuing to encourage them to hold onto the unique power of the warrior identity.

More Stuck than Broken

Large numbers of my fellow warriors are wrongly getting slapped with the label "broken." Too many of those who begin to embrace such a faulty label never fully make the transition to a fulfilling civilian life. They get stuck between worlds and so cannot move into the full, satisfying life they both deserve and want. I wrote *The Warrior Dilemma* to help all warriors avoid getting stuck between these two very different worlds.

Please understand, I have *no* desire to diminish the importance of working clinically with significant combat-related stress injuries or other mental health pathologies! These problems are very real and need to be addressed appropriately.

At the same time, a very large percentage of veterans who do not meet the criteria of some specific mental health pathology nevertheless are going through treatment as if they have one. Such treatment has not, will not, and cannot give them the help they need. Something much deeper is not being addressed.

I have not set out to write a long treatise, so please forgive me if some of my statements seem brusque or terse. I want to get straight to the point so that you can identify current issues that may be causing difficulties in your life or in the life of a friend, and then suggest how you can begin to make some necessary, even lifesaving changes.

Finally, please don't write me off if I write something you disagree with or identify as "not my struggle." If you are a warrior making the transition to the civilian culture, I guarantee that the things discussed *will* apply to you. Too many warriors use the excuse "civilians don't get it" to avoid the key issues negatively affecting them. The two most intellectually lazy people are those who reject everything they hear and those who accept everything they hear. It takes effort to figure out what things apply to you.

While you may not agree with everything I state and while some issues I discuss may not apply to you directly, most of them certainly will apply. Take those pieces and adapt them, if necessary. The goal is to get ready for the transition. Do not underestimate how impactful it can be!

Let's get started.

1

★ ★ ★

Common Problems

The problems are not always caused by what you might think.

Just like we would with an operations order, we need to start by examining the situation many have struggled with, perhaps for years. Consider this chapter a situation report. While it may seem morbid, it provides us with necessary understanding.

Too many of the active-duty warriors I work with believe they will encounter very few problems once they leave the military. They expect to excel without issue the moment they re-enter the civilian world. Often, however, within a few months or years, many of them find themselves struggling desperately to find their places outside of the military.

This may not be you! But I encourage you to think, as you've been trained, to "plan for the worst and pray for the best."

Multiple Transition Problems

Multiple problems commonly plague the veteran trying to transition into the civilian world. Unfortunately, many of these warriors are told that Post Traumatic Stress Disorder (PTSD) lies at the root of their transition difficulties, which saddles them with a great stigma they may find difficult to overcome. The civilian world tends to consider PTSD not only a disorder, but a disabling one at that. Civilians may question if the veteran is going to "go off" at some point.

As I've worked with veterans trying to transition back into civilian life, I have identified many serious problems besides PTSD that create tremendous difficulties. The four of the most important ones.

1. Suicide

Without question, suicide tops the list. Most veterans and active-duty service members recognize that suicide has touched all their lives. Not all of us will become suicidal, of course, but many do struggle here, so we need to address the issue. It's also important to recognize that the suicide epidemic among veterans does *not strictly* depend on the combat veteran's combat exposure. Let's look at some research that reveals the enigmatic nature of this problem.

While the high suicide rate of veterans is often attributed to PTSD, research shows that such a diagnosis alone does *not* lead to higher suicide rates.[i] The comorbidity of PTSD and other disorders, such as depression, are much more highly correlated with suicide. In fact, depression is *the* dominant cause of a high suicide rate among veterans, whether they saw combat or not. Suicide rates among non-combat veterans is just as high as those among combat veterans.

One study conducted by the Pentagon revealed that in a given year, 52 percent of suicides by active-duty service members involved individuals not deployed to combat zones. Such a statistic startles many who hear it. "I have no reason to think that way," say many warriors. Some studies claim that the high suicide rate can be traced in part to childhood issues that were left unresolved until after the soldiers left the military. While that may be true in some cases, an additional and powerful activating factor is in play for most veterans.

Too many times I have heard some warrior say of a buddy who committed suicide, "I never thought he would be the type of person to do that." The deceased warrior was often considered an excellent performer who did his or her job well. Many looked up to the individual and gave him or her great respect. Those left behind wonder, *What would get such a quality person to the point of even considering suicide as an option?*

2. Violence

Many veterans also have significant problems with intimate aggression. The

VA has training that helps providers understand that intimate aggression (both physical and verbal aggressive actions toward loved ones) among veterans is double the national average among the civilian population and quadruple the rate among combat veterans. Obviously, this puts tremendous strain on relationships and swells the rates of relationship failure—and a primary precipitating event of suicidality is failed relationships. A recent study reported that 52 percent of suicides among veterans was due to relationship failure; second was legal and vocational problems.[ii]

This observation comes out of more than academic research. Over my years of working with warriors, the primary activating event for most suicidal veterans I have worked with has been relationship distress or loss. Intimate aggression, expressed most often through anger, is usually the chief complaint of the spouse and eventually leads to the breakdown of the relationship. Why is this such an issue for the warrior community?

3. Parenting

A veteran's perceived abuse of his or her children is another common problem. After warriors leave active duty, many of them see child abuse cases getting filed against them. Why? You should understand this critical situation if you are transitioning away from active duty.

Military culture is much more aggressive than civilian culture. It's also much more willing to use corporal punishment to adjust undesirable behaviors. Military service members and veterans, therefore, often repeat in their homes the same type of discipline they expected from their unit or subordinates. Veterans parenting their children as if they were in the military can cause serious problems.

For an outside observer, such behavior may seem harsh and even abusive, especially in states with strict child abuse laws regarding physical discipline. Neighbors or members of the surrounding community, often those working in the medical or psychotherapy fields, often file official complaints with civil authorities. I have seen many veterans ordered to take court-mandated therapy when they came under investigation for some type of Child Protective Services (CPS) violation. To appease the courts, they must work on their parenting skills and provide some evidence of improved behavior.

Some warriors overreact to their children making mistakes. Why? Most of us take *all* performance mistakes very seriously. From boot camp on, we are taught that mistakes get people killed. If mistakes in combat get warriors killed, the outcome for survivors is drastic or even tragic.

Many warriors regret their harsh response to their young children who make some simple mistake. We often justify it because of our conditioning, meant to prevent greater catastrophe. Such harsh treatment in the home often causes children to fear making any mistakes at all. Such fear usually impairs a child's performance in school because the educational system is all about making mistakes and learning from them. The warrior culture, by contrast, does its best to prevent mistakes, due to the catastrophic outcomes indelibly imprinted in our minds. A failure to treat mistakes differently in the civilian and military worlds often creates serious problems for our children and legal and relational problems for ourselves.

The warrior community also tends to produce children who rebel in their teenage years, usually due to harsh discipline they received in their formative period. In the warrior culture, discipline is paramount, and relationship is secondary. The military routinely erects barriers to limit relationships between leaders and subordinates. The Uniform Code of Military Justice (UCMJ) still includes penalties for fraternization with lower-ranking subordinates. Many parents from a warrior culture begin to look at their children as if they are subordinates and treat them as such. Such a shift usually happens subtly.

The military encourages a "subordinate mindset," emphasizing the proper role of separation, so that leaders can make better decisions and appropriately dispense discipline. Good reasons exist for the military to limit leadership's relationships with subordinates.

Such a mindset becomes a great problem, however, when warriors discipline their children without fostering deeper relationships at the same time. Disciplining children without building relationship creates rebellion. It is *relationship* that bonds children to their parents, not duty or chain of command. Parents who fail to cultivate deep relationships with their children, even while disciplining them, will watch their children rebel against the discipline and against their parents, especially as those children grow older. The warrior community has a legal structure that keeps subordinates from rebellion, but the family has no such legal or communal consequence for rebellion. A failure to recognize the difference between the two cultures continues to create heartaches and regrets for warriors who raise their children with a military mindset rather than a parental one.

4. Legal Problems

Time and again, I've seen veterans reach rock bottom when they get into some type of legal trouble in the civilian world. I've seen many veterans get placed on probation for some legal infraction and have watched many others enter the legal system when charged with making "terrorist threats" after they gave a neighbor an ass chewing for rudeness or inconsideration to the community. Or maybe a veteran sought a thrill, trying to outrun police on a motorcycle, only to realize later that while they lost the police, they could not outrun their license plate. I have seen decorated warriors run into innumerable legal issues after exiting the military.

> A failure to recognize the difference between the military and civilian cultures continues to create heartaches and regrets for warriors who raise their children with a military mindset rather than a parental one.

Legal problems are exacerbated, of course, by alcohol-related incidents. Time and again, I see veterans ordered to get therapy after altercations in which they acted aggressively and were charged with assault or a DUI. With active-duty service members, the military culture usually can shelter its own from civilian consequences. Veterans, by contrast, usually suffer the full weight of the consequences of their illegal actions. Thankfully, veterans' courts and diversion courts often give warriors a chance to expunge their record.

While this does not minimize the fact that legal situations pose a substantial problem for veterans transitioning back into the civilian world, it does beg the question, "Why do so many warriors run into so much of this trouble after their military service?" Too many of us blame it on PTSD, which may contribute to the problem, but many who do not have PTSD still struggle with these issues. So again, what is it about the transition from the warrior culture to the civilian culture that makes this such an issue?

A Significant Problem

Not all veterans struggle with this transition and many do not fall into the traps of the key problem areas just outlined. Still, a significant number of warriors *do* struggle with the transition, and many of them cannot make the transition on their own.

I hope that the information in this book will help to make you more aware of a significant problem that we must address. The difficulty of re-entering civilian society does not always correlate with PTSD or another mental health disorder. In fact, the very things that made us feel like powerful warriors in the military may create significant problems for us in the civilian world. How does this work? It all starts with how we became warriors in the first place.

Pass and Review

- Not all problems that come from the transition to civilian life are driven by disorder.
- Suicide is only a symptom of the problem, and it affects more than combat veterans.
- Aggressive responses create multiple problems for the transitioning warrior.
- Parenting style can become a problem for warriors when entering the civilian world.
- Legal difficulties are a normal pitfall for transitioning warriors.

Inspection

1. How have you seen others struggle in these areas?
2. In what areas already discussed do you believe you have the greatest tendency to struggle?
3. Do you believe that you are beyond many of these problems? Explain.
4. What would you do if some of these problems began showing up in your life?
5. Where would you go for help or support?

★ ★ ★

PART ONE

The Warrior's Conditioning

2

★ ★ ★

The Making of a Warrior

*The Transformation is much deeper and longer lasting
than any of us ever anticipated.*

What causes the biggest issues for military personnel transitioning out of the armed services? Why do so many warriors struggle so deeply with re-entering the civilian world? It's important at this point to set a basis for understanding the overarching problem.

I do not believe that something new and profound is taking place in warrior history. We are experiencing things that have taken place in all warrior cultures in all ages, at least to some level. Nevertheless, our current warrior culture does have some unique nuances that differ from previous warrior cultures. Let's look briefly at the history of the American warrior to give ourselves a fresh perspective from which to examine what's happening with so many struggling veterans today.

A Change of Perspective

Today's American warrior culture is not made up of draftees or those forced into military service. We have an all-voluntary force whose members see value in such service or are looking for some greater purpose or meaning in life.

Our country takes pride in being able to field an entire fighting force without requiring anyone to be drafted. At the same time, such a shift creates some potential consequences. I have worked with combat veterans of several eras and have noticed a significant difference in warriors today regarding a willingness to accept the military's psychological transformation. Vietnam-era warriors weren't necessarily opposed to the war-fighting psychological conditioning, but as draftees, they saw it as necessary for going to war and coming home alive. It was not a personal life decision, but more of a decision of duty and honor. This type of entrance into the warrior culture changes the receptivity to the conditioning.

An all-volunteer force subtly changes the mentality of the culture.

If you are a warrior, you already grasp what it means to be one, but perhaps you have not defined it clearly. Let's start by understanding what defines a warrior. For the purposes of this book, a warrior is an individual who has enlisted his or her life for the service and protection of others who cannot protect themselves.

In her book, *The Code of the Warrior*, Dr. Shannon French explains that warriors separate themselves from civilian culture because they are willing to live under a higher standard of conduct and even sacrifice themselves for a higher cause. This is important because at the core level of a warrior culture, the individuals separate themselves from the civilian culture. The question is, if they separated themselves for a greater purpose, how do they later rejoin the culture from which they intentionally separated themselves?

Not long after I began my academic work in psychology, I began to recognize the depth of the psychological transforming/conditioning I went through in the military. I've heard many warriors say that while they didn't find boot camp, especially difficult physically, psychologically it was grueling. Psychological conditioning is a critical component in transforming civilians into warriors, a process both intentional and powerful. I doubt we fully appreciate how changed warriors are from the civilians we once were.

We often assume that because we came from civilian culture, we will easily re-assimilate into it. Such an assumption tremendously underestimates the power and depth of the warrior transformation. Many warriors throughout history who have re-entered civilian culture would express how difficult and complex such re-assimilation can be. Many books written by warriors testify to the difficulty of the task. Let's break it down for a better understanding.

A Potent, Deliberate Process

The military has become adept at psychological conditioning. Lieutenant Colonel Dave Grossman wrote a popular book titled *On Killing* that landed on the commandant's reading list for the Marine Corps. Grossman compellingly demonstrates how we have improved our ability to condition our war fighters to minimize their hesitation at taking another human's life. He breaks down how the military has done this using many psychological and behavioral conditioning techniques.

> **Quick note:** Some people react adversely to the term "conditioning" because they feel it has a negative connotation. I do not use the term to describe the common conception of "brainwashing." As used throughout this book, it describes the necessary tool that all warriors must submit to for the required internal and external transformation process. This must take place for civilians to become warriors, or none of them would return alive to their homes.

Consider one simple example from Grossman: Changing the shooting target from a basic circle with center mass to a human silhouette. Repeatedly shooting at such a target creates a behavioral pattern, conditioning the shooter to look at a human silhouette in the sites of his or her weapon and repeatedly pulling the trigger. Grossman highlights this activity as an important "killing" conditioning exercise for modern warriors. And it's not the only conditioning taking place. At the same time, multiple areas are targeted to transform the civilian into a warrior.

Grossman is not the first individual to recognize this issue, of course. A salty old Marine highlighted the same kind of psychological conditioning many decades before:

> "Boys with a normal viewpoint were taken from the fields and offices and factories and classrooms and put into the ranks. There they were remolded; they were made over; they were made to 'about face.' They were put shoulder to shoulder and through mass psychology they were entirely changed. We used them for a couple years and trained them to think nothing at all of killing or being killed. Then suddenly, discharged and told them to make another about face. This time they

had to do their own readjusting without mass psychology, without officers' aide and advice, without nationwide propaganda. We didn't need them anymore. So we scattered them about without any speeches or parades. Many, too many of these fine, young boys are eventually destroyed mentally, because they could not make that final 'about face' alone." [iii]

A highly decorated Marine named Smedley Butler wrote those words back in 1935. He received the Medal of Honor twice for gallantry in combat and retired as a Major General. At the time of his death, he was the most decorated Marine in U.S. history. Although he wrote these statements in a time of peace in the nation, notice some of the terminology he used: "mass psychology," "remolded," "entirely changed." He also declared that little to no effort was made to undo this radical transformation.

Butler wrote almost two decades after World War I and a few years before World War II broke out, yet even then he movingly described this profound transformation from civilian to warrior. He also emphasized the consequences of failing to adjust to such wartime conditioning after the soldiers returned home.

Almost a century later, I can assure you that our mass psychology has vastly improved over the years! A former naval officer who now helps Navy Seals transition from the military highlights this point:

"I was unaware that I was being psychologically conditioned. I think that the department of defense, and the military in general, is very good at removing obstacles from people so that they can accomplish the mission. The goal really is about accomplishing the mission and not about the individual. It has to be about the mission. So, they have to train us to put mission before self, which is a very unnatural process." [iv]

Please don't see my statement as criticizing the practice of conditioning citizens to be warriors, because that would betray the warrior. We train our warriors in this way so that they can effectively operate in a combat scenario when the lives of their brothers and sisters (and their own) are on the line.

Our military has no interest in creating problematic psychological issues for warriors. Rather, it strives to make and condition civilians into warriors who want to serve in one of the world's premier fighting forces. It has no malicious intent behind such training. It remakes civilians into warriors to prepare them to fight the nation's battles so that the United States may remain a free country.

Nevertheless, a great disservice *is* done to those warriors when the conditioning they undergo is not "undone" once they leave the military. This sabotages their efforts to re-enter and successfully navigate civilian life.

Don't Underestimate the Challenge

So much goes into the making of a warrior! Many of our nation's military services proudly proclaim that they will transform young people into warriors, but most of us vastly underestimate what this means from a civilian perspective. I doubt that even we warriors recognize the depth of our transformation until we try to re-assimilate into a civilian environment—and transitioning from military to civilian life does not typically go well for warriors who underestimate the situation facing them.

> Transitioning from military to civilian life does not typically go well for warriors who underestimate the situation facing them.

If we think of being a warrior as "just a job," things begin to backfire on us. A regular job does not ask you to sign away your life for several years (more on this later). We also do ourselves a great disservice when someone asks how we could successfully handle some tough combat situation, and we reply, "I was only doing my job." Regular jobs don't ask of you what the warrior culture demands from you. The impact can also last a long time. One former Infantry Marine described to me a powerful experience he'd had:

> "At an event for my first job after I got out, I was at a college representing an energy drink. As I was interacting with others there were these two girls from a Muslim background. They blew me off and made fun of me. I said, 'That's okay, I don't serve rag heads anyway.' One of these girls heard me and her parents own liquor stores that carried this energy drink. They called corporate and I got fired over it.

"I was in the office with the manager and her manager above her, and they were chastising me. They didn't even try to understand me. I know people would think, *Oh, you were just out to verbally assault and demean Muslim people. You were just out on a rampage.* No, I wasn't. When I was in the military, that's just how we were conditioned to talk about Muslim people. When we went to Iraq, we were already using the term Haji and rag head; it was part of the culture. I'm not gonna lie, man. I think part of it, psychologically, made shooting them easier. It made fighting them in a war easier.

Now, all of a sudden, I come back and any time I use those terms, I get crucified. 'I just went off and fought a war for you!' I'd yell. You fire me from the job for use of that terminology, the same terminology that we had to use to make it easier to identify and kill our enemy.' I sat there with the boss and her boss in the office, and they were chastising me and giving me their little speech about being verbally insensitive, acting like they were better than me. I just lost it.

"I said, "You know what? I know you don't understand me. I don't expect you to. I'll tell you something: it's the very people you vilify, like me because I used an unacceptable word, who went out and fought on your behalf so you could even have your little energy drink company."

This is just one example of how the conditioning we go through can impact our transition into the civilian environment. I've heard thousands.

As we begin to explore how the military transforms civilians into warriors, we must recognize that the armed services have mastered the use of operant and classical conditioning, as well as identity and cultural conditioning (which can be even more powerful). I will describe various examples of how the military uses these strategies to mold a warrior's behaviors and actions, and how similar strategies are used to develop military discipline. Without understanding how these strategies work and how they are employed, most warriors will find it very difficult, if not impossible, to transition back to civilian life.

When we seek to answer the question, "What makes the warrior transformation so powerful?" we must first understand some key concepts about identity, because identity is at the heart of being a warrior. After I began working in this field and had seen hundreds of veterans, I began to understand that identity is a crucial element of the transformation, with or without PTSD. I then began to study what elements form an individual's identity.

While what follows is not an exhaustive list, it describes what I have come to see as significant in the formation of one's identity. As you consider several key areas, you will likely begin to see how *your* warrior conditioning powerfully impacted your own sense of personal identity.

Six Pillars of Personal Identity

Let's take a brief look at six of the most important pillars that form an individual's identity. More than likely you will resonate with some more than others, but all of them play a part in building one's personal identity.

1. Existential or Spiritual Meaning

This element probably lays the foundation of a person's identity. It begins with the fundamental question of the purpose of one's existence. All of us, either philosophically or pragmatically, begin answering this question as we develop through adulthood. The meaning we land on can be as simple as "survival of the fittest" or "being created for the glory of God." The worldview you hold influences how you judge an individual's value. Personal life experiences obviously contribute to development in this area.

2. Family/Personal History

How do you identify with your own history? This can form on an individual basis (personal successes and achievements), but it seems to have the most power when passed down generationally. Families with a rich history of producing medical professionals, for example, or families with a strong history of producing professional athletes, tend to have significant traits and habits that get passed down from one generation to the next.

Unfortunately, this doesn't hold true only within positive family backgrounds, but also within more negative backgrounds (as many can attest who have worked with populations with histories of domestic violence). Negative behavior can just as easily get passed down the line because hurtful behaviors and tendencies naturally reproduce themselves through modeling and example.

Family histories, whether positive or negative, have significant power to help form an individual's personal identity.

3. Cultural history

A culture's history can directly influence a person's identity. We see a clear example of this when we observe Texans. I served with many Texans. If you know any Texans, you know that they personally identify with the state, even to the point of getting the state flag tattooed onto their body. They highly value Texas and what it gives them, which greatly influences their identity.

As we will see, military culture has a profound influence on a warrior's personal identity. Ponder some of the ways your own military experience has deeply influenced how you see yourself as a person.

4. Personally Held Values

One's value system has a tremendous influence on the development of personal identity. We naturally identify with the things that we believe or hold dear. You reveal what you value through how you spend your time, energy, or money. When you see what a person values, you will begin to see who the person really is.

If somebody is patriotic, for example, their value system is grounded in some form of strong identification with their country. This value influences their preferences and how they deal with problems. Most faith practices have a deeply held value system that strongly influences how believers identify themselves. The military very precisely and extensively uses this pillar of identify formation.

5. Natural Talents and Passions

I list these together, as one typically follows the other. Natural talents help to build your identity because some natural skill you have commonly elicits praise and accolades. If you are very fast and can easily catch objects thrown your way, you may like to play football, and soon your identity begins to form around that area. Or you may be very intellectual and astute, and quickly you begin to identify yourself within a more cerebral arena. Passions typically follow natural talents, as they elicit strong emotions of excitement or concern, creating a strong internal drive to pursue some outcome or make an impact in some area. What you feel passionate about affects how you identify yourself.

In most cases, passions and natural talents go together. If you are good at a sport, you often become passionate about it. Think back over your own life. Recall the things that you felt passionate about or did very well. More than likely, you identified with these things in some way and used them to help you form your personal identity.

6. Convictions (Promises You Make and Keep)

At first, I found this concept difficult to conceptualize. It became more real to me, however, as I saw how it played out in my own military experience and as I witnessed the same thing occurring in the lives of hundreds of others.

Our identity began to form around the continually repeated idea that "the promises you make are the promises you keep." I have relabeled it here as "convictions" because I find that unkept good intentions and promises never help to form one's identity. If, however, your good intentions and promises get put to the test—when you must persevere and exert strenuous effort to keep those promises—they become convictions.

This is a crucial area of identity formation. When your promises get put to the test and you must sacrifice to keep them, they have a strong impact on the way you begin to view yourself. If you are a married man, for example, and you feel tempted when an unknown woman hits on you—but you hold strong to your commitment to your spouse—you begin to identify yourself as a committed married man. If you compromise your commitment, however, you will not identify yourself as a committed married man. Almost certainly, the latter decision will negatively affect your personal identity.

Moreover, the more you compromise your integrity, the more your actions will splinter your identity. The term integrity is often used to describe the wholeness and sound structure of a ship. In a similar way, when you make and keep your promises, your integrity grows and you become more whole and sound as a human being. Can you see why the military so strongly pushes integrity? The warrior culture puts one's promises to the test.

> The formation of personal identity is critical to understand if we are to observe what takes place during the warrior transformation.

I've spent a little extra time on this issue because the formation of personal identity is critical to understand if we are to observe what takes place during the warrior transformation. It may help to reflect over your own experience in the military. Keep your radar up for these areas as we turn to an exploration of the specific techniques the military commonly uses to make a warrior.

Pass and Review

- Warrior cultures must transform civilians into warriors.
- Conditioning is the means of the transformation.
- Conditioning is not easily undone and profoundly impacts the warriors' future.
- Identity is at the heart of the transformation process.

Inspection

1. What is a warrior and how and why do they differ from a civilian?
2. How have you seen the warrior culture condition you?
3. What conditioned responses do you think will create (or have created) problems for you in the civilian world?
4. How has the military impacted your key areas of identity?
5. If you are not an active warrior, how do you identify yourself?

3

★ ★ ★

Behavioral Conditioning

The transformation starts with stripping and a complete rebuilding..

When the military sets out to re-form a recruit's identity, the first thing it does is to make sure that the recruit's former identities don't get in the way. Before the military begins to inject the warrior identity that it wants to instill in all recruits, it has to begin to "prep the target."

Without question, one of the first tasks the military sets out to accomplish is to strip away the civilian identity that the recruit has taken eighteen to twenty years to develop. (I use that age range because it's the average age of recruits entering boot camp.). This is where the transformation process begins.

> One of the first tasks the military sets out to accomplish is to strip away the civilian identity that the recruit has taken eighteen to twenty years to develop.

Strip to Equal

The first step in stripping away a recruit's civilian identity is to remove identifiable personal traits. Two simple actions have an oversized effect.

1. Get a haircut

Most of us recall getting marched down to have our heads shaved or given a standardized haircut as a "welcome to the military" event. I'm sure that many reasons are offered for doing this to recruits, both sanitary and pragmatic.

But by shaving a person's head, you remove one of the most obvious things that distinguishes one individual from another.

It comes as a great surprise to see how similar everybody looks when they all have a shaved head (except for those poor individuals who look especially pathetic or alien with no hair; we all knew a few of those). While female recruits do not shave their heads, all of them must have their hair cut to a minimal length and continue to wear it in a uniform style.

There is nothing new to this tactic. Throughout history, when one culture wanted to dehumanize or shame another, the more powerful culture has shaved the heads of its subjugated adversaries to depersonalize them. This is a powerful tool that is used to strip the identity from the individual. Please, don't minimize the psychological impact of this action on a young adult!

2. Remove all civilian clothes and artifacts

After the head shaving comes the removal of all the recruit's civilian clothes and artifacts. They will not be seen again until the warrior transformation is complete.

Other services do this differently than the Marine Corps, but in all branches of the military there is some kind of a putting away, even for a short period, of the civilian identification created through individual clothing choices and other personal effects. Everyone is issued the same clothing and gear, differentiated only by slight size variations. That includes if you were one of the unlucky ones issued the BC (birth control) glasses. I believe I stated that I did not need glasses, just to avoid the shame.

Many private schools follow a similar pattern in requiring students to wear standardized uniforms. Because most civilians value variety and differentiation, students at these schools often manipulate their uniforms to create some type of individuality. When a recruit enters the military, however, no such uniform manipulation is allowed. Why not? Individuality is in the process of being extinguished for the sake of cohesion and uniformity. This is one of the deeper areas that must be deconditioned when a warrior transitions back to civilian culture .

Strip Personal Worth and Value

I lack both the time and the space to begin listing the creative and ingenious ways that drill instructors use to make recruits feel like a lesser form of life than civilians working on base. Let's focus on just one of these ways—the eliminating of personal space.

All of us hold tightly to personal space as a basic human right. Although the amount of personal space desired varies by culture and individual, when it is breached, the affronted person takes offense.

Recruits entering boot camp are required to stand in a line called "A to B," which essentially means one person's ass touches the next person's belly-button. Everybody lines up in this manner. Why? This technique eliminates personal space and becomes a stripping-down method.

When recruits need to use the bathroom, again they find personal space eliminated. If you can't picture this strategy, imagine a bathroom with only ten urinals that a fifty-member platoon has the use of for just thirty seconds. Not thirty seconds per platoon member, but thirty seconds for the *whole platoon* to finish its corporate business (let your imagination picture the chaos). I still remember five or six guys crowding around one urinal, all of us trying not to pee all over ourselves, because if we did, we would be shamed for soiling our uniform.

Even though every recruit enters boot camp as a civilian, this stripping of identity quickly makes them all feel as if being a recruit they have given up their personal dignity. I still remember sitting in the barber's chair. After weeks of such conditioning, I felt as though those barbers were somehow above me as human beings.

The military employs many similar methods and techniques to strip recruits of their civilian identity, but this should be enough to illustrate the point. The military does this intentionally so that recruits will be "clean" to receive the warrior identity.

Such techniques have been used throughout history, often employed as punishment in internment or prisoner of war camps. They have proven very effective in stripping away personal identity, even to eliminate a prisoner's will to fight.

Our military uses a similar strategy to strip away a recruit's identity, but not in a punitive way (even though that is exactly how it looks and feels as you go through it). Those of us who were transformed into warriors by this process realize that such steps are necessary to create effective war fighters. While the methodology does not produce the intended results for 100 percent of recruits, it almost always works extremely well for those eager to embrace the warrior identity.

Here's the bottom line: *The stripping of a recruit's personal identity is crucial to forming a warrior.* The more completely the past identity is removed, the more open the recruit is to receive a stronger identity, a warrior identity. I have seen the power of this stripping away process, even if someone tries to resist it. One warrior distinctly recalls this process and the feelings correlated with it:

> "I still remember phase one of boot camp when they were tearing us down. I remember going in to get a haircut and the civilian barbers would push your head around to the right angle, and they would do it in a way that you could only count it as a sense of disdain. They were obviously encouraged to do this by the drill instructors.
>
> "The subtle message when you are stripped down from an identity is that you begin to feel less than the civilian. I didn't understand it: just four weeks earlier I was equal to the civilian, but now that I was a recruit, I was a lesser form of life than the civilian who was now shaving my head. I felt a level of shame just by being in his presence."

Everyone Needs an Identity

Something inside of us always wants to identify with something bigger outside of us. We all have an internal vacuum that we try to fill. Some try to fill it by identifying themselves through hobbies or music or sports or clothing or the like. As trivial and shallow as some of these identities can seem, they often go impossibly deep. Late adolescents typically come into the military with fragile identities that do not hold up to the stripping process.

It's also worth noting that many young men and women come into the military trying to escape their identity, often connected to dysfunctional families or difficult situations. Those who come from troubled homes often join the military to flee or to get a fresh start. Many young men and women come from great households, of course, and from families that instilled in them the virtues of duty and service. Still, those who join the military to get away from past identities tend to be *far* more open to embracing the warrior identity than others.

All humans, and especially adolescents, seek an identity that feels meaningful. When boot camp strips away the old identity, a vacuum is created. Drill instructors are more than ready to fill that vacuum.

The stripping of personal identity is the first step in the transformation to warrior. Without this (often demeaning and painful) process, barriers would remain to accepting the new warrior identity that the military wants soldiers to have for at least the next four years. Once the old identity has been stripped away, recruits are more open to receive the warrior identity designed to equip them for future war fighting.

> All humans, and especially adolescents, seek an identity that feels meaningful. When boot camp strips away the old identity, a vacuum is created. Drill Instructors are more than ready to fill that vacuum.

Operant and Classical Conditioning

The terms "operant" and "classical" conditioning are used to describe the ways various situations can be used to condition an individual's psychological response. The common term used to describe this type of conditioning is "brain washing." We all have thoughts that come to mind when we think of this term, but it simply is meaning the conditioning someone goes through to get a psychological and physical response. Boot camps are full of these practices.

Drill instructors will startle recruits awake and then expect them to operate and react effectively despite the stress of their unexpected awakening. Such a boot camp conditioning method starts to prepare new soldiers for combat when they must always be ready to go into action immediately. Countless examples of such classically conditioned responses exist throughout boot camps. And how does this relate to identity?

At some point in boot camp, a recruit moves from being viewed as a "less than" human to the initial phase of becoming a Marine/Soldier/Sailor/

Airman. A shift takes place somewhere in this rebuilding, occurring through the completion of simple tasks such as wearing one's uniform in an appropriate manner. Recruits reach little milestones as they progress through boot camp, each one giving them more freedom. Maybe they can begin to blouse their boots (tuck their pants into ankle holes to create a balloon-like effect), clearly identifying them as a Phase 1 recruit. As they progress further and move into later phases of boot camp, they earn further opportunities to show their status, signifying that they are getting closer to becoming a warrior. At one significant point, they get their name taped on their uniform. This simple action has a profound effect in getting them to identify as a service member.

These details are *much* more than little rewards; they become key milestones that work together to build a recruit's new internal identification. They prompt the recruit to want the official title even more and create a deep hunger to be personally identified as a warrior.

When recruits first enter boot camp, they can hardly follow *any* drill commands for marching. Yet as they move on and compete for the best marching platoon, they begin to take pride in and feel a part of something bigger than themselves. Many observers wonder why in the modern era the military continues its emphasis on marching. They miss a larger factor.

Beyond mere tradition, marching teaches young military trainees a tremendous psychological lesson. They learn that their actions, if out of sync, negatively affect the whole. Marching ingrains in them the mental mindset that they are one in purpose and movement, emphasizing importance of unit cohesion and uniformity. Through marching and the cohesion and uniformity it demands, recruits build a basis of identity. Uniformity begins to become more important than individualism.

Marching also creates a basis for the military discipline of "instant, willing obedience to orders." Drill requires immediate response to the order of the commander. It provides the foundation for all future conditioning of warriors. Within the structure of the unit, personal identity is built. One former drill instructor states:

> I think of it now—the conditioning we do on the drill field and why we "destroy" kids. And these are the words we use: "Oh yeah, absolutely destroy kids." These kids understand there are ramifications for

inaction on incident-based orders, but they're never going to get it and they're never gonna get better. They're never gonna become part of the team. No, they're going to be an individual.

So, it's breaking down the individual's thought process to finally say, "Okay, it's not about me. It's about team. And I'm over here getting destroyed because I did it for me and not for them." Once you break them of the individuality—not taking away their personality, but the mindset of being an individual on everything that they do— then you replace that with a team mindset. That's when you start to see the platoon form.

Can you begin to see why removal from the structure in which the warrior identity was formed is such a huge issue for warriors leaving the military?

Basic training uses many forms of behavioral conditioning to equip service members for combat. Many veterans have told me of having to learn in boot camp how to do certain absurd activities. Only after they arrived at their first unit and received more combat-related training did they suddenly realize those "absurd" things had been designed to condition in them certain automatic behaviors. Many of the repetitive tasks they were required to do had been instilled for a greater purpose.

To better understand how this works, let's investigate a key component of the way the human brain functions. It will give us a fundamental insight that the warrior culture has used for thousands of years.

Muscle Memory's Four Levels of Learning

The military uses behavioral conditioning to create automatic responses in cases of life-and-death situations. Maslow's Hierarchy of Learning helps us to understand the process used by the military to create these automatic responses in its warriors.

1. Unconscious incompetence

The first step recognizes that *we don't know what we don't know*. Most of us who entered the warrior culture had no idea how complacent and ignorant we were regarding potential threats. We had hardly more idea regarding the fundamentals of handling guns and other lethal forms of weaponry. We didn't know how incompetent we were. Most of us started right here when we joined the military. We had no idea what it would take to become a warrior. We had no clue what was about to transpire. It's a good thing that our superiors refused to leave us in this state!

2. Conscious incompetence

At this second step, a recruit becomes aware of a deficiency in some area of his or her understanding. On a very basic level, the military starts with recognition of rank insignias correlating to one's hierarchy in the new environment. It soon becomes much more complex than this.

At this stage, many recruits learn the fundamentals of handling a weapon safely. They become aware of how negligent in handling the weapon they either had been in the past or would have been in the future. They become aware of their level of incompetence. While that's crucial, they can't stop here, because it's just enough to make them a danger to themselves and others.

3. Conscious competence

At this stage, recruits become aware of the proper way to do things, and then they actively discipline themselves to operate in this way. Recruits intentionally try to handle their weapons safely. This usually becomes a learning process in which drill instructors catch their mistakes and help them to remember the correct way—typically through a little pain. Adding pain tends to help the process move more quickly to the next level of learning.

At this stage, the recruit is able to compete the task, but only with effort and conscious thought. Warriors cannot settle for this stage, because too many things can go wrong if they must stop and think about some reaction.

4. Unconscious competence

Warriors at this stage do not have to consciously remind themselves to apply the competence and understanding that they sought to gain in Step 3. For the safe handling of a weapon, warriors get to a point—with many hours of painful reminders—where they can handle a weapon safely without even thinking about it. It finally becomes "muscle memory."

This type of competence occurs in many of the warrior's job components, regardless of his or her Military Occupational Specialty (MOS). For the infantryman, this means practicing immediate action drills over, and over, and over, and over again. Many infantryman often become annoyed with such continuous and repeated practicing, but after a first combat experience, you will hear many of them talk about how the "training just kicks in." This "just kicking in" experience happens only because of instructors who spent much time and effort building unconscious competence into their warriors. The same process takes place in most areas of a warrior's job and life.

Leaders and instructors work hard to condition this "muscle memory" response because when actual combat begins, such conditioning works against the survival mechanisms innate in every human. When an individual would naturally try to hide from harm, this conditioned response kicks in to move that individual *toward* harm to neutralize the threat. When weapons fire, the conditioned warrior moves toward the gunfire rather than away from the gunfire, in opposition to the innate self-preservation response.

A healthy majority of military training is built upon this premise, so that when a life-and-death situation comes, the warrior doesn't even have to think about it. He or she just acts in the way the training dictates. This is the bread and butter of the behavioral conditioning methods used by the military to condition warriors for intense combat.

Still, it's just the first level in making a civilian into a war fighter.

Pass and Review

- Before the warrior identity can be placed, the civilian identity must be removed.
- Our military has mastered the science of stripping personal identity.
- The transition from the individual mindset to the "we" mindset is critical to the warrior identity.
- Muscle memory is intentionally conditioned to created automatic behaviors.

Inspection

1. How did it feel to have your civilian identity stripped away?

2. What were the ways that you experienced the stripping of your identity? Don't pass this by; take time to remember your experience.

3. What was the most impactful way you remember of transitioning from an individual to a team mindset?

4. In what areas of your life do you still see an automatic response instilled from the military?

4

Existential Conditioning

The foundation of the warrior transformation is instilling the ethos.

While behavioral conditioning helps to make a civilian into a warrior, several other types of conditioning lie at the heart of the transformation. This more complex conditioning is what truly makes warriors.

While behavioral conditioning focuses on repeated actions to create habitual behaviors, more complex conditioning addresses the warrior's basis of thinking itself. This type of conditioning begins to work from the inside of the warrior rather than from the outside.

Shannon French studied many warrior cultures to prepare to write her book, *The Code of a Warrior*. She insists that warriors in these cultures are not simply fighters, killers, or mercenaries, but have something within them that takes everything to a much deeper level. The name "warrior" holds tremendous meaning for civilizations that exalt warriors.

If the military trained its service members using behavioral conditioning alone, it would create fighters, but not warriors. Warriors need more than just training; they need to be transformed through a makeover of their internal being. For lack of a better term, I call this "existential conditioning." While the term falls short of the full scope of factors involved in this transformation, for this book I will use it to identify this crucial aspect of transformation in the making of a warrior.

How crucial is it? Existential identity conditioning is probably the most powerful and profound tool for transforming a citizen into a warrior. Behavioral conditioning can get a person or animal to behave in desired ways by applying the right stimuli, but getting them to keep such a mentality without instilling it into their very character is very difficult. Some behavioral conditioning remains embedded in their behaviors, but without existential conditioning, the spirit is missing. If certain behaviors are forced upon them but never personally held by them, they will seek to extinguish those behaviors once the external influences have disappeared.

> Existential identity conditioning is probably the most powerful and profound tool for transforming a citizen into a warrior.

A very different phenomenon takes place in the military. Warriors are consciously instilled with a strong identity that compels them to act and behave in certain ways. If you are about to leave the military, be sure that you will find many things in the civilian world that you will disagree with or even detest. If you're already out, then you know this reality firsthand.

So, what do we do about this existential conditioning? First, we must know how it works. The key question then becomes, "What did the military do to change civilian identity into a warrior identity?" The warrior culture does this through four primary avenues: the warrior ethos, the warrior code, the warrior's purpose, and the warrior's suffering. In this chapter we'll investigate the warrior ethos. In the next chapter we'll look more closely at the other three avenues that the military employs to change civilians into warriors.

Ethos Conditioning

If you have been in the military, no doubt you have often heard the term "warrior ethos." Sometimes you took it seriously and other times it was said in jest. Understand, however, that the warrior ethos has a powerful effect on the transformation process.

How potent? I know that I did not fully grasp its power when others worked to instill it in me. But whether we sense its power or not, we must come to see why it plays such a critical role in making a civilian into a warrior. Let's begin with some definitions.

The warrior ethos comes from the individual creed that guides the warrior and determines valued conduct and/or attitude. It also encompasses a deep, personally held view of ourselves. In other words, it is a prescriptive way to assign future conduct for yourself. Even though you may not yet have had to live out the standard, you set your mind and spirit to follow through with it. Warrior cultures define this ethos in different ways, but they all reflect this spirit.

How, then, does the warrior culture condition this type of massive internal transformation?

1. The beginning: Swearing in

The military begins to instill this warrior ethos at the "swearing in" when a civilian enlists. Any warrior can tell you about the time they first joined the military.

Potential recruits visit a military enlistment center (MEPS) to get checked for physical fitness of duty. Some make it no further; a physical or psychological disability eliminates them. If they pass this initial screening, they enter a room to be sworn in. Most young recruits are not ready for the sacred and somber process of this experience.

The ceremony begins with recruits raising their right hands and swearing upon their lives that they will defend the Constitution against all enemies, foreign or domestic, even to the point of giving their own lives. They quickly realize they have walked into something sacred and very serious. The experience is eye-opening for most of us.

Most of us don't often take this type of sworn oath upon our lives. The vast majority of civilians will *never* take such an oath. While members of other professions, such as medical professionals and law-enforcement personnel, take other oaths, the military oath stands out. It says the U.S. government can use an oath-taker however it sees fit, even to the point of death. Such an oath is not used in civilian culture. Hence, taking the oath makes the moment much more decisive to a young adolescent.

Ask an ex-military friend about his or her own swearing-in experience. Many will remark how serious it felt for them when they walked out of the room. Without question, making a personal oath of this magnitude has a profound impact on your identity. One warrior told me:

"Oh man, when I swore in, I was like, *Oh shit, what did I just do?* I had never had to swear in at court or anything like that. Now, I just had to raise my right hand and swear my life over to my country. I don't think anybody could prepare me for what the seriousness of that felt like. It dawned on me after that moment that I had just committed myself to something that I cannot back out of."

When the "promises that you make are the promises you keep," you greatly impact the formation and solidification of your identity (remember "The Pillars of Identity"). Regardless of whether we knew it at the time, by making such a big promise, we began the process of becoming warriors. The warrior culture we joined would certainly hold us to our promise (or expel us through a dishonorable discharge if it felt we did not fulfill our obligation).

If you're a veteran, recall how you made this oath. Remember how many times someone held you to this oath, or how superiors told you to go to places you didn't really want to go. Reflect on how taking the oath obligated you to give up the freedom to direct your own life. Every bit of that began with this oath.

Oaths have a powerful influence on the formation of the warrior ethos. The commitments and promises you made—and more importantly, how you followed through with those commitments and promises, sometimes to your own harm —profoundly affected your self-identity. If you are a warrior, you understand that you will take no other oath in life that will have this high of a potential cost.

2. Ingrained communal history

Not all military services equally practice this aspect, but all services do greatly reference their history, at the very least through museums and textbooks. And some services take their history very seriously.

Marines, for example, are not allowed to move to the next phase in boot camp until they pass a test on Marine Corps history. They must memorize details about the founding of the Marine Corps, as well as the tremendous battle history of Marine warriors who have gone before them. Don't make light of this step because it is important for the existential conditioning.

All warrior cultures instill in their new members the history built before they arrived. Remember that how you personally identify with something bigger than you *greatly* impacts your own personal identity. The warrior culture ties your personal history to its organizational history, and its history is not your history. A prime example is the annual "birthday balls" that celebrate the origin of your specific warrior culture. Those balls become part of your history.

Marines have a long-celebrated tradition in which every year the commandant gives a message. Every year he recalls many of the epic battles that Marines have fought over the proud history of the Corps. All commandants remind Marines that this is now *their* legacy. They carry forward this battle history into their contemporary conflicts.

The Marine Corps hymn, which all Marines memorize and sing in unison, is based primarily on the Corps' battle history: "From the halls of Montezuma to the shores of Tripoli, we will fight our country's battles in air, on land and sea." The Marine Corps does this to ingrain this identity into its young service members. It truly instills a personal identity connected to the Marine combat legacy.

All military organizations instill their history of service into their recruits because they know it encourages the recruit to personally identify with that specific military service. Don't think of this as some stagnant recounting out of a history book without a dynamic connection to the military history of which you are a part. To identify with an organization in this way has a powerful impact on the warrior ethos. A combat-hardened Marine commented on this facet of his conditioning:

> "Maybe it's just the lineage of the Marine Corps, all those guys and gals in all the wars from the inception of the Corps to the present, that we do have this tenacity that is unparalleled. If you look at the medal of honor citations, the Navy cross citations, if you just look back through the hands of time and remember all these wars and what the Marines went through—the frozen chosen, to Vietnam—all of these things. There's a distinct delineation between reading about a Marine, the Marines fighting in that war and reading about the Army fighting in that war. Like, holy crap, these guys literally walked in and said, 'Okay, I did that today.' But that's what I signed up for. They went all

the way to death. We recognize that. And do you feel like that's part of your history? Yes.

3. Esprit de corps

You hear this term a lot in boot camp. It refers to the invigoration and motivation for the unit, the mission, and one's personal identification as a warrior.

Initial entry into a warrior culture always greatly emphasizes personal motivation. I remember hearing it from my earliest days, when more senior recruits would encourage me by saying, "Stay motivated, recruit." I did not realize at the time that such personal motivation was intended to help form my identity. Remember, the things you feel passionate about will begin to form your personal identity.

We see this in the early motivation of warriors. Many young warriors, after graduating from basic training, will wear their T-shirts back home or even get a tattoo reflecting their personal motivation. We endearingly call these "boot tattoos." This aspect gets challenged once a warrior makes it into the "fleet," but often makes a strong resurgence after leaving the military. I know this simply by observing all the unit T-shirts, operator hats, and stickers on vehicles I see every day just going to work.

All of this goes back to the simple principle that whatever you feel passionate about is how you self-identify. Many of us didn't realize all that the military provided us until we got out, and then it was gone. *Esprit de corps* is a great thing to keep morale up; this may be the very reason the warrior culture takes such pains to instill it in recruits. But it also has a crucial secondary effect on the individual warrior, functioning as a potent form of existential conditioning and one more building block to instilled identity.

4. Value system

Most significant of all is how the warrior culture shapes the value system of its warriors. This reflects yet another pillar of identity. One's identity formation is powerfully affected by what the person values, his or her value system.

All of us grew up with some type of value system, whether structured or unstructured. When you enter a warrior culture, however, you find a very different value system, one very intentionally put in place.

Many of us do not realize that once young warriors swear in, they are willingly indoctrinated into the creeds of their service. All military branches have a primary creed that sets in place the value system for every individual warrior in that branch. Consider the creeds of the four main service branches and notice the value systems those creeds express. Look for the values being impressed:

Soldier's Creed

I am an American Soldier.
I am a warrior and a member of a team.
I serve the people of the United States and live the Army Values.
I will always place the mission first.
I will never accept defeat.
I will never quit.
I will never leave a fallen comrade.
I am disciplined, physically and mentally tough,
trained and proficient in my warrior tasks and drills.
I always maintain my arms, my equipment and myself.
I am an expert and I am a professional.
I stand ready to deploy, engage, and destroy the enemies
of the United States of America in close combat.
I am a guardian of freedom and the American way of life.
I am an American Soldier

———————————— ★ ★ ★ ————————————

Airman's Creed

I am an American Airman.
I am a Warrior.
I have answered my Nation's call.
I am an American Airman.
My mission is to Fly, Fight, and Win.
I am faithful to a Proud Heritage,
A Tradition of Honor,
And a Legacy of Valor.
I am an American Airman.

Guardian of Freedom and Justice,
My Nation's Sword and Shield,
Its Sentry and Avenger.
I defend my Country with my Life.
I am an American Airman.
Wingman, Leader, Warrior.
I will never leave an Airman behind,
I will never falter,
And I will not fail.

★ ★ ★

The Sailors' Creed

I am a United States Sailor.

I will support and defend the Constitution of the United States of America and I will obey the orders of those appointed over me.

I represent the fighting spirit of the Navy and those who have gone before me to defend freedom and democracy around the world.

I proudly serve my country's Navy combat team
with Honor, Courage and Commitment.

I am committed to excellence and the fair treatment of all.

★ ★ ★

My Rifle
(The Creed of a United States Marine)

This is my rifle. There are many like it, but this one is mine.

My rifle is my best friend. It is my life.
I must master it as I must master my life.

My rifle, without me, is useless. Without my rifle, I am useless.
I must fire my rifle true. I must shoot straighter than my enemy who
is trying to kill me. I must shoot him before he shoots me. I will.
My rifle and myself know that what counts in this war is not
the rounds we fire, the noise of our burst, nor the smoke we make.
We know that it is the hits that count. We will hit.

My rifle is human, even as I, because it is my life. Thus, I will learn it as a brother. I will learn its weaknesses, its strengths, its parts, its accessories, its sights and its barrel. I will ever guard it against the ravages of weather and damage as I will ever guard my legs, my arms, my eyes and my heart against damage. I will keep my rifle clean and ready.

We will become part of each other. We will.

Before God, I swear this creed.
My rifle and myself are the defenders of my country.

We are the masters of our enemy. We are the saviors of my life.

So be it, until victory is America's and there is no enemy, but peace!!

———————————— ★ ★ ★ ————————————

As you read these creeds, note the significant value systems expressed through them and impressed by them. These creeds reinforce to the individuals reciting them that they are now committed to an organization that will force them to live by these creeds, or they will be disciplined accordingly.

These creeds not only instill a kind of righteous fear in those who recite them, but also help to ground the personal identity of each warrior in the ethos of the creed. Many young adults long to have something to identify with, and the warrior culture will gladly fill that longing.

Creeds, by the way, do not end with the initial creed of whatever service a recruit may join. Creeds are built upon and refined. If you were in the military, recall the other creeds you learned as you advanced. All of them were meant to influence you. Specific roles often come with new creeds. Most services have creeds for officers or for becoming a staff noncommissioned officer. The Marine Corps has an oath for becoming a noncommissioned officer and a staff noncommissioned officer. These build as you take on more leadership and only more deeply ingrain the value system in you. I realize that many do not live up to all the standards of these creeds, but the value of "what ought to be" is still present, even if the individual is not living it.

And the creeds do not stop there! If you move into a more specialized unit, you will have creeds that instill values above and beyond the primary military creeds. Two specialized units, for example, have unique creeds for their elite warriors. Consider the following specialized creeds for Army Rangers and Reconnaissance Marines.

The Ranger Creed

Recognizing that I volunteered as a Ranger, fully knowing the hazards of my chosen profession, I will always endeavor to uphold the prestige, honor, and high esprit de corps of the Rangers.

Acknowledging the fact that a Ranger is a more elite soldier who arrives at the cutting edge of the battle by land, sea, or air, I accept the fact that as a Ranger my country expects me to move further, faster and fight harder than any other soldier.

Never shall I fail my comrades. I will always keep myself mentally alert, physically strong and morally straight and I will shoulder more than my share of the task whatever it may be, one hundred percent and then some.

Gallantly I will show the world that I am a specially selected and well-trained soldier. My courtesy to superior officers, neatness of dress and care of equipment shall set the example for others.

Energetically will I meet the enemies of my country. I shall defeat them on the field of battle for I am better trained and will fight with all my might. Surrender is not a Ranger word. I will never leave a fallen comrade to fall into the hands of the enemy and under no circumstance will I ever embarrass my country.

Readily will I display the intestinal fortitude required to fight on to The Ranger objective and complete the mission, though I be the lone survivor.

Rangers lead the way!

——————————— ★ ★ ★ ———————————

The creed that still gives me chills on the back of my neck whenever I repeat it is the Reconnaissance Creed. I am a Recon Marine and I had to thoroughly memorize these words while in basic reconnaissance course.

The Recon Creed

Realizing it is my choice and my choice alone
to be a Reconnaissance Marine,

I accept all challenges involved with this profession.

Forever shall I strive to maintain the tremendous reputation
of those who went before me.

Exceeding beyond the limitations
set down by others shall be my goal.

Sacrificing personal comforts and dedicating myself
to the completion of the reconnaissance mission shall be my life.

Physical fitness, mental attitude, and high ethics—
The title of Recon Marine is my honor.

Conquering all obstacles, both large and small,
I shall never quit.

To quit, to surrender, to give up is to fail.

To be a Recon Marine is to surpass failure;

To overcome, to adapt and to do
whatever it takes to complete the mission.

On the battlefield, as in all areas of life,

I shall stand tall above the competition.

Through professional pride, integrity, and teamwork,
I shall be the example for all Marines to emulate.

Never shall I forget the principles
I accepted to become a Recon Marine.

Honor, Perseverance, Spirit, and Heart.
A Recon Marine can speak without saying a word
and achieve what others can only imagine.

Many more military creeds exist for various units, divisions, and specialties. I hope you see the significance of the value systems being instilled into every warrior that adheres to these creeds. Some may consider creeds nothing more than words on a page, but for the warriors who have sweat in training and bled in war, these creeds are *far* more than mere words. These creeds carry on the battle legacy of all those who came before us. These creeds also give warriors a standard by which to conduct themselves, high standards that separate them from civilians.

> What a shock for warriors to return to a culture that completely lacks any communal creed designed to instill higher standards of conduct! It can feel like trying to swim in a lake completely drained of water.

I cannot emphasize enough how impactful these creeds can be for a warrior—especially when that warrior leaves the military and re-enters civilian life. What a shock for such a warrior to return to a culture that completely lacks any communal creed designed to instill higher standards of conduct! It can feel like trying to swim in a lake completely drained of water.

An Enormous Impact

The warrior ethos is one of the most powerful factors in identity formation, in part because it becomes so personally held. It also has a significant confidence-boosting effect. Not all warriors adhere to the warrior ethos, I know. But whether they like it or not, it did have an impact on them at some level.

Those who truly embraced the warrior ethos, which includes a good majority of warriors, continue to be tremendously impacted by it, long after leaving the military. It probably will affect their personal identity for the rest of their lives.

When I ask Vietnam and World War II veterans to name the top five of their most significant formative experiences, their wartime experience almost always makes the top three. Countless times I have heard others say, "I don't understand this. It happened more than fifty years ago. Why do they continuously want to think and talk about it?" Numerous senior warriors want to get together to discuss and reflect on one of the most significant experiences of their lives. They consistently tell me that no one understands them like the other veterans in their group.

When I asked a former 1st Sergeant to describe how the military had affected his identity, he said:

"I have become institutionalized, and the military thought of that. And then, just recently, I retired, with all the struggles I go through. I am institutionalized and conditioned to exist inside of a certain world. External from that world, I feel exposed and vulnerable and just bewildered. All my sensors are off-kilter. The military absolutely conditions you, some good, some bad, some whatever. You're not just a Marine; you are in a whole subculture of America, a small subculture, and it infiltrates all aspects of your life.

My wife has been conditioned. She was living with this for twenty years, of me being a Marine. She's conditioned, my children are conditioned, to a degree. My entire family knows only being a Marine, on a Marine installation, in a Marine environment, with other Marines, Marine wives, and Marine children.

Does the warrior ethos continue to play a key role in their lives? You tell me.

Pass and Review

- The warrior ethos lies at the heart of the warrior identity.
- No oath is like the oath you take when you give your life over to the military.
- Your personal history is intertwined with your unit's/organization's history.
- Where your passion/motivation is, your identity will follow.
- Your values form who you are and who you will become; your creed brings them together.

Inspection

1. What was swearing in like for you?
2. Identify the warrior creed with which you most identified. What elements of the creed still resonate with you?
3. If you have been in the civilian world, what have you seen there that some would consider a creed?
4. Examine your creed to see if it will continue to work for you, now that you are in the civilian world.

5

★ ★ ★

Missional Conditioning: The Warrior Code

The codes of warriors are what separates them from civilians.

While the warrior ethos plays a potent role in forming the personal identity of most warriors, it doesn't work by itself in the arena of existential conditioning. Three other elements play an equally powerful role in shaping and solidifying a true warrior's personal identity. Each of the three have some significant connection to mission, so with this chapter, I begin our discussion of them under the label of missional conditioning.

The warrior *code* finds it foundation in the overarching mission of the warrior, the focus of this chapter. The warrior *purpose* finds it meaning in the primary mission of the warrior, which we will consider in the next chapter. And the warrior *suffering* finds its camaraderie in the pain usually required to complete the warrior's mission, which we will look at in Chapter 7, Cultural Conditioning.

Let's take a look at the warrior code and its impact on service members leaving the military.

The Warrior Code

The warrior code is communal in nature. It overlaps the warrior ethos but has a different application. The warrior code refers to the outward standard by which the community holds and reinforces proper or acceptable conduct, whereas the warrior ethos refers to the internal value system that influences an individual's conduct and integrity. The warrior ethos is personal; the warrior code is communal. They overlap, but both play a distinct role in the transformation of a civilian into a warrior.

All military services have a warrior code, both written and unwritten. The official code is published and posted in some official form, while the unwritten code is communicated and enforced in a more unofficial way by the community.

Core Values

The warrior code for most services is called "core values," which usually differ from the warrior ethos. These core values are communally enforced and are expected to be personally held. The Marine Corps, for example, has the core values of honor, courage, and commitment. From my generation to the current generation, Marines usually receive an honor, courage, and commitment card, about the size of a credit card, to put in the soldier's wallet. Marines are to carry it at all times to remind them of the core values they are supposed to uphold. Even an off-duty warrior somewhere in town can be challenged by other Marines to show honor, courage, and commitment.

I teach a class to warriors just out of the military. The first time they come to class, I ask any former Marines present if they still carry their card. Multiple Marines always show me their card, even though they're no longer in the Marine Corps.

Marines are taught that honor is synonymous with moral and physical integrity, which plays out in the honesty they exhibit. Integrity is a significant communal expectation. This most often comes out when they are expected to do something they committed to do, even though no one may be watching. Many warriors have gotten themselves into significant trouble, and even handed a non-judicial punishment (NJP), over an integrity violation. The warrior culture takes integrity very seriously and can punish the lack of it with communal shaming.

> If you know a warrior culture, you know the communal force that can be applied to live by its code, and the shame that comes if a warrior fails to live up to it.

If you know a warrior culture, you know the communal force that can be applied to live by its code, and the shame that comes if a warrior fails to live up to it. Integrity is critical to identity because it holds you accountable to actually live out the core values.

Formalized Military Rules

The Uniform Code of Military Justice (UCMJ) is a set of formalized rules and regulations that form the military's legal system. Those of us who have lived under this code clearly understand it, but for the civilian who may be reading this, a brief explanation is in order. The UCMJ spells out the standards of conduct that, if violated, lead to punishment, whether through loss of pay, loss of rank, or even loss of freedom (restriction).

The standards and regulations of the UCMJ are much higher than civil legal codes. It has regulations on height and weight, for example, stipulating how a warrior can be punished for failing to meet those standards. The UCMJ says a warrior can be charged and punished simply for failing to obey the orders of a direct superior. If a captain tells a private to be someplace at a certain time, for example, and the private does not show at that designated time, the warrior can be charged with a violation of unauthorized absence (UA). Even though no specific regulation stipulates time, if a warrior fails to follow an order giving a designated time, he or she can be charged with failure to obey an order.

On a more ethical level, the military still commonly charges and even forces warriors out of the military for adultery. This makes sense, especially when you consider a culture whose members spend long periods away from their loved ones. The impact of adultery on a family unit distracts the team from its mission focus. Adultery is considered a betrayal among military service members and usually is dealt with harshly. In order to keep their heads in the game regarding some mission objective, warriors must have confidence that when they leave home for long periods, the family and loved ones left behind will remain faithful.

The UCMJ details many more infractions in its communal code that often exceed the civilian code. This is important that it does exceed the civilian code, which we will discuss later. But for now, understand that the

UCMJ is meant to express a high standard of conduct and behavior. The code/UCMJ is all about external forces that instill a personal drive to obey military standards.

Unit Traditions and Roles

Any given unit also has its own traditions and rules that it enforces on its own. Unit traditions have a history of being passed down from one generation to the next, to the point that the unit treats the tradition as more sacred even than the UCMJ.

Traditions can vary between different types of units. For the Marine Corps, tradition is treated as sacred. An example is the Marine Corps Ball, which every year celebrates the Marine Corps' birthday on November 10. This ball is steeped in tradition, from the cake cutting to the listening of General Lajune's speech. The whole formal tradition is held in reverence . . . until the end of the last part of the ceremony, when the drinking begins and the reverence leaves.

A less formal tradition forbids Marines from walking on grass, usually in garrison. Marines get it drilled into their heads that walking on grass is against the rules.

I'm not sure of this tradition's value, but no Marine questions it. One day I walked with an active-duty Marine in a civilian environment after leaving a meeting on a college campus. To get to our cars, we had to cross a small section of grass. As we neared the grass, my active-duty friend said, "You're going to do it, aren't you? I can tell, we're walking directly at it." I immediately knew what he was talking about, of course, because we continued to walk straight toward the section of grass beyond which sat our parked vehicle. I watched as he looked around to make sure nobody saw, and then he begrudgingly and with clenched teeth walked across the grass with me.

I had reconditioned myself to jettison this rule because I regularly visited multiple college campuses, all of which had large sections of grass and very few sidewalks. Even so, when I glance at some building I have to reach, sometimes, I still have an automatic reaction against crossing the grass. It may seem comical, but it shows the power that traditions have for those who have served in units that enforce such rules. These traditions are designed to instill a habit of obeying the code.

Why a Higher Standard?

The warrior code is meant to maintain a higher standard than what exists in the civilian world. This code—from the ethical, to the civil, to the tradition-al—is designed to exceed what is expected of mere civilians. French's *The Code of the Warrior* states that what universally defines a warrior culture is its code of standards that exceeds what exists among the civilian populace. This code separates warriors from civilians, both in conduct and in ethics.

And why is this so important?

First, you must understand another concept. Why do civilians sometimes actively put themselves in harm's way for other civilians? Some significant conditioning must have occurred, whether religious or ethical. Consider the phenomenon of civilian adults willingly sacrificing themselves or putting themselves in harm's way for a child in distress.

My neighborhood has a busy street, and when a civilian saw an unattend-ed three-year-old wandering next to it, she immediately stopped her car and ran to the child to keep that child from running into the street. Next, she went on a vigilant search to find this child's home. While this is not an espe-cially abnormal action for a responsible adult, what compels such a person to try to protect an unknown young child? Deep inside, the adult knows that young children cannot protect themselves, so the adult feels compelled to act on their behalf.

One of the most powerful forms of conditioning that exists is the separation required to make a civilian into a warrior. The codes that warriors swear to uphold make this distinction powerful. A higher standard of expectation has an enormous impact on the warrior psyche. Think about that for a moment. Do you see the parallel?

> The impact of the word 'code' separates the warrior from the civilian to such a degree that warriors begin to think of themselves as a more equipped and powerful form of human.

The impact of the word "code" sepa-rates the warrior from the civilian to such a degree that warriors begin to think of themselves as a more equipped and powerful form of human. As demeaning as that may sound to a civilian, it is a crucial psychological mindset for every warrior.

When warriors are trained to hold themselves to a higher standard than the civilian populace, they separate themselves from those civilians. This separation places them psychologically in a higher status than civilians. This is how you train young warriors to willingly put themselves in harm's way for others. The conditioning is designed to build the mentality that warriors alone possess the ability and the power to protect those who can't protect themselves.

In a very popular video released in 2003 just before a Marine battalion entered Iraq, a lieutenant gives a speech to his men. In the speech, the lieutenant motivates his men by saying they are going to protect those who cannot protect themselves. This same type of speech has been given thousands of times before entering harm's way. Let's examine this conditioning.

The military conditioned its warriors to feel above mere civilians, so that they would willingly sacrifice themselves to protect those civilians—and our warfighters do a damned good job at it. But what happens to those warriors when they leave the military and its warrior culture? Can they just "turn off" their conditioning once they return to a civilian setting? Hardly. It makes sense why so many warriors have a very hard time fitting in after they get out of the military. Yet so many believe that they will get out and walk right back into the civilian world without skipping a beat.

But now, throw in the real catch 22. Even if the military *tried* to recondition its warriors to re-enter civilian society, who wants to take on a lesser identity? Warriors are conditioned to believe they're "above" civilians— that's why warriors need to protect them—and who willingly chooses to give up their superior mental state just to feel like you are just a civilian again?

In Part 2 of this book, we'll address the question, "So what are we supposed to do now?" Before we get there, however, let's continue our quest to better understand the identity dilemma that warriors commonly go through.

Who Enforces the Code?

For most military services, a service member who picks up the initial leadership rank/billet is expected to be the first-line enforcer of unit traditions and rules. This role varies in major military services. In the Army it can be an E-5; an E-6 in the Air Force; but in the Marine Corps, it is usually formalized as a corporal/E-4.

Most Marines know that a Corporals' Course (formalized school of initial leadership) is in session whenever they see corporals wandering around the camp, looking for transgressors of the warrior code. These corporals often notify other Marines that they are out of sync with the regulations.

As warriors grow in leadership, they are expected to enforce the regulations and code and set an example for others. This provides another reminder that the code is enforced communally, which gives it greater impact than if only the legal authorities enforced it. The warrior code gains much deeper significance within the warrior community when the community itself holds its members accountable.

So, what do you think happens when someone leaves the military and settles in a place without any widely understood communal code held to by neighbors (or anybody on the freeway)? We don't realize how important the code is until it isn't there.

Don't miss how vitally important it is for warriors to have a code by which they live. A warrior's code has existed among all significant warrior cultures; it is of primary importance in the warrior culture. I would say it's what makes a warrior culture a culture at all.

No warrior has a code without also having a purpose—which brings us to the next building block of the warrior's identity.

Pass and Review

- The warrior community always has a code meant to elevate the conduct of the warrior to a higher standard.
- Integrity is a critical component to securing the warrior code and instilling it into the warrior's identity.
- The UCMJ is made to reflect a higher standard of civil conduct than most civilian counterparts.
- The warrior culture is a tradition-based culture because it instills both codes and reverence.
- A warrior must feel superior to civilians in order to sacrifice for them.
- Without a code, the warrior would have no culture.

Inspection

1. What feelings do you recall about separating yourself from the civilian culture?

2. What traditions in your military unit(s) were the most meaningful for you? Why?

3. What parts of the military codes that pertained to you stand out as different from the civilian culture?

6

Existential Conditioning: The Warrior Purpose

The loss of purpose is one of the most difficult things to live with.

Neither the warrior ethos nor the warrior code can take full effect unless they also have "the why." Without the why, everything else becomes trivial, even meaningless. The warrior purpose is the glue that holds the code and the ethos together.

While *purpose* is the most significant driving factor for warriors, I believe we tremendously underplay how powerful it really is for warriors living in the military culture. I hear civilians say to warriors all the time, "It's good to be part of something bigger than yourself, and you did something to be a part of it," but many of these civilians never get to feel the full power of such an experience. While many believe they are part of something bigger, they never get the potent experience that comes from *fully* acting out a greater purpose, which most of the time comes only by way of great sacrifice. One retired warrior reflected on the power of purpose:

> "I felt a hundred percent purpose, like from day one in bootcamp. I knew what my purpose was. I had some good leaders and some crap leaders, but the purpose was able to get me through this. My purpose was absolutely to make myself as proficient as I possibly could at whatever my craft was. You'll be doing everything from being a cook to the front man on the firing line in whatever war. It didn't even matter, because there is a purpose."[vi]

We All Need Purpose

People often assume that a warrior's general sense of purpose for serving in the military is also what drives the warrior culture. While it certainly plays a part, it does not supply the complete motivation. In general, you can discover the underlying purpose merely by asking a simple question: "Did you *serve* in the military?" or "Were you in the *service*?" The very question implies that the person's purpose for being in the military was to *serve* our country.

While this truth supplies only a small fraction of what it means to have a significant purpose in the military, it does give a basic description of the military's fundamental nature: to serve the nation. This has been a powerful force of purpose throughout many generations and in many nations.

In his book, *Man's Search for Meaning*, Victor Frankel highlights how many of his fellow Jews in a Nazi concentration camp quickly died after they lost their sense of meaning and purpose. Frankel later established a whole therapeutic orientation that addresses the importance of having a purpose in life. He is most famously quoted as saying, "A man can get through any what, if he knows the why." He established how important it is for humans to have a life purpose, and how they tend to lose the will to live when they lose their sense of purpose.

Humans need a purpose to live. The absence of purpose often leads to some level of depression. The extreme worldview of nihilism holds that both the world and human existence are meaningless; there is no purpose to find. This worldview has never attracted a wide following, mainly because so many who adopt it struggle with depression or self-destructive behavior.

The conditioning we went through in the military capitalized on this internal drive for purpose. It is the nature of the profession. When much is on the line that cannot be won without significant sacrifice, a psychologically appropriate reason must exist for continuing to push forward. Military service naturally has an intense sense of purpose that differs from most civilian experiences of purpose. The intensity of military life and the great sacrifice it requires mean that warriors must adhere to the purpose more robustly.

Suppose you visited an amusement park and rode only the Ferris wheel. You knew nothing about the other rides. This would be a satisfying experience. But if you then rode some intense, upside-down roller coasters, and afterward returned to the Ferris wheel, you would become acutely aware of what you'd been missing.

And so it is with warriors who return to the civilian world. When they re-enter the society they left and then try to accept the primary purposes behind most civilian life, they often feel empty. The "why" they find in society cannot compare with the deeply meaningful purpose they had in the military. This often leads to great frustration for veterans trying to re-assimilate into a civilian environment.

> "When warriors re-enter the society they left and then try to accept the primary purposes behind most civilian life, they often feel empty. The 'why' they find in society cannot compare with the deeply meaningful purpose they had in the military.

If you are getting out of the military, be prepared for the impact of this significant loss in your life. Consider a conversation I had with a former Force Recon Marine. "Once you got out," I asked him, "Did you notice a loss of that sense of purpose and significance?"

"Oh yeah," he answered, "you go from every day waking up knowing that what you're doing is for your team, for your platoon, for your command, for your unit, for your country. Everything that you do, you're doing it for something." He continued:

"And then, all of a sudden, you come home and it's like everything that you do, you question: 'What is this? What is the significance behind this?' I'm waking up today, but there's no mission. There's no purpose.

"Okay, I ask myself, 'What have I learned?' Well, I've learned that I need to stay in shape. So we go to the gym, we keep ourselves physically fit, we're going to stay strong here. So, I'm going to continue to exercise. But then it's like, when I do it, what am I doing it *for*? Oh, you know, you're doing it for yourself. You're physically fit. Yes. For your health. Yes. But in the military, you did it for the higher purpose to be combat-ready, to be able to perform in a combat scenario when lives are at stake. But now, it loses something. It's different.

"Then, you go to work or to school. I started going to school and I am always asking myself, 'What is this really for?' Ultimately, it turns into trying to set goals and trying to reach those goals. You're working to reach those goals. But what if those goals will never overshadow the purpose that we had in the military? It is a step down. I think a lot of times veterans get really discouraged by that. I know I do."

This warrior concluded, "Our reason to live is not as powerful as it once was."

How Does the Military Create Purpose?

All of this should make us ask, "How does the military create such a deep sense of purpose?" Outside of its overarching purpose to serve, the military environment supplies multiple levels of purpose, which often intentionally overlap.

The kinds of purpose you find depend on the branch of service you join. The Air Force has a very different purpose in carrying out its mission from the Marine Corps. While the overarching mission is the same for both services (to serve), each has specific roles to play, with very different purposes.

The further down you go from the overall purpose of whatever branch you joined, you find increasing refinement. It eventually reaches the specific service member's Military Occupational Specialty (MOS). The MOS gives individuals clarity on their duties and role in the larger organization. A basic infantryman has a very different specific purpose than a helicopter mechanic. Both, however, are very clear on that purpose and what it means to the bigger mission.

Your purpose can get even more refined than your MOS, based on your type of unit. A communications operator's purpose looks very different from an infantry unit than with a logistics unit.

Additionally, purpose comes not only from your job, but also from your role as a leader in that job. Leadership often adds very significant identity aspects in the warrior culture and can greatly impact how significantly a warrior identifies with purpose. I have seen twenty-three-year-old men become fire team leaders or squad leaders and lead twelve other warriors into highly kinetic combat scenarios. They may never get to experience anything remotely like it in the civilian world. Such leadership responsibility greatly impacts the individual. Without question, this type of experience solidifies a warrior's internal drive for a sense of purpose, as one Afghanistan veteran explained:

> "I felt like I did have a purpose, especially going up in rank because I had to take care of somebody. I always had somebody I had to take care of. I either had to go wake up my fire team leader or I was the fire team leader. I had to get my boys up earlier. The squad leader had to get my whole team up. I had to make sure everybody was up. I was always looking after somebody and that gave me my sense of purpose. I viewed it like, 'I have to help these guys. We have a mission. We have to protect our country.' It's that simple.

When you are in the warrior culture, your purpose becomes intertwined with the big picture and the bond that you have with others. Part of serving your country overlaps with taking care of those who serve with you.

That drive intensifies when warriors lose a buddy in combat, because their mind longs for a sense of purpose and meaning to help cope with the loss. The greater the purpose, the more help they find in making meaning of the loss. I've often worked with warriors after the loss of a fellow warrior in combat, and their minds want to find some greater purpose to help them create meaning and so make the loss worth the sacrifice. Even though a strong sense of purpose does not bring back the deceased comrade, it gives a level of dignity to the death.

A dear friend of mine who died in combat in 2006 kept his last letter to his family in his left breast pocket, to be sent to them only if he was killed in action. He understood this point and expressed it in his letter:

> "Here's something tangible. What we have done in Iraq is worthy of any sacrifice. Why? Because it was our duty. That sounds simple. But all of us have a duty. Duty is defined as a God-given task. Without duty, life is worthless. It holds no type of fulfillment. The simple fact that our bodies are built for work has led to led us to the conclusion that God put us together to do his work. His work is different for each of us."[vi]

Dan knew that clearly stating his purpose would help his family and friends grieve his loss. Notice that the *principle* of what he was doing, and not its *outcome*, was the main factor driving him.

When a warrior cannot find meaning in this type of loss, a sense of grief often follows that typically morphs into survivor's guilt. Purpose is an extremely powerful tool, especially when dealing with the extremes of war. The warrior culture needs purpose to help warriors cope with the consequences of war.

A Clear and Potent Purpose

The purpose that a warrior feels, even in a few short years of military service, can be more significant than in most areas of civilian life. It is not that civilian life lacks meaningful purposes, but that those purposes are not as clear or as potent as they tend to be in the military.

In the military culture, one thing is very clear: you are part of a bigger purpose and you know your specific role in that purpose. Of course, many military service members feel frustrated regarding their purpose, but I have found that most of them felt deeply frustrated when they were not being *used* according to their purpose, not because they did not *have* a purpose.

Many of us have seen the movie *Jarhead* about a Marine sniper doing everything he can to fulfill his sniper mission and get a confirmed kill. The movie highlights his perspective and the great frustration he experiences because he is never able to complete his mission. At the last moment he has an enemy in his sight, and he is told to hold off so that close air support could be used instead. He felt great frustration that he could not fulfill his purpose. Hollywood got hold of the story and exaggerated certain elements, of course, but the film still illustrates the fact that Marines can experience this kind of deep frustration when they can't complete their assigned mission.

> Warriors who identify with their purpose and who personally own this sense of purpose find that it greatly impacts their personal identity. Most warriors do not realize how much they have gained from this clear and potent purpose until they no longer have it.

When most of us joined the military, we imagined ourselves as fighting machines. We soon came to the harsh realization that we would be fighting machines only when we were deployed to combat zones. Much of the rest of our time we spent cleaning and police calling. I've heard many of us say, "I joined the military to be a war fighter, and now I feel like a janitor." All of us, at some point, had our frustrations when the bigger purpose for which we joined the military was not lived out in daily life.

Warriors must understand the vital importance of this idea. Warriors who identify with their purpose and who personally own this sense of purpose find that it greatly impacts their personal identity. Most warriors do not realize how much they have gained from this clear and potent purpose until they no longer have it.

At times, of course, politics and other forces cloud the purpose that we felt for our being in and fighting in a foreign country. This does not mean that we didn't find a purpose. Every warrior must come to some conclusion about his or her purpose in the military, even if they don't fully understand the stated purpose.

One Vietnam veteran shared in a short story how he coped with this reality: "This was a crazy, fucked up war. It seemed it was being waged far more for political reasons than for any other purpose, so I decided my only real mission and number one priority was to get those I was responsible for safely back to their families and loved ones."

Even if you don't understand the overall purpose of why you are fighting, every warrior needs a clear purpose so that he/she can fight for it.

When Purpose Leads to Pain

When someone has a strong purpose that brings meaning and direction to their lives, they will sacrifice for that purpose. And what is a sacrifice? The dictionary answers, "The surrender or destruction of something prized or desirable for the sake of something considered as having a higher or more pressing claim."[vii]

Purpose often leads to sacrifice—and sacrifice usually involves suffering of one kind or another, to one degree or another. In what may seem counter-intuitive, the more communal pain we suffer together, the stronger our personal connections typically grow. Shared pain and suffering tend to produce especially strong bonds that form in no other way. This reality can make the journey from warrior to citizen especially hard for many service members leaving the military.

Pass and Review

- We all need a sense of purpose; it is innate to the human experience.
- One of the greatest losses for veterans leaving the military is the loss of being part of a much greater purpose.
- The military culture creates levels of refined purpose (MOS, billets, leadership) that deeply ingrain into the warrior the meaning and clarity of that warrior's purpose.

Inspection

1. Recall the sense of purpose and pride you had when you graduated bootcamp. What made your accomplishment so special to you?
2. What was your purpose in the military? Have you ever experienced any type of equally significant purpose in another area of your life? Explain.
3. What is your purpose now?

7

★ ★ ★

Hardship Conditioning: The Warrior Suffering

Our suffering together breeds the depth of our camaraderie.

Pain and suffering usually serve as the primary catalysts the military uses to ingrain ethos, code, and purpose into the warrior's identity. We don't have to like it, but suffering as a group fosters deep, personal, internal connection. We see this phenomenon not only in the military, but in many aspects of life.

A Reunion of Sufferers

Those who endure significant tragedies together often hold reunions where they gather periodically to reminisce with one another over their shared experience. People who have survived difficult times in life, and who during that time connected in some significant way with others, tend to create lasting bonds with the individuals who went through the difficulty with them.

> We don't have to like it, but suffering as a group fosters deep, personal, internal connection.

Maybe they made it through extreme two-a-day football practices in the hot and humid summer to kick off a championship year. Or perhaps they were study partners who prepared together for the grueling exams they had to pass to complete a difficult program. Or yet again, every year as September approaches, we see announcements or news articles describing how survivors of the 9/11 terrorist attacks plan to get together for reunions. Whatever the situation, the more significant the suffering, the more significant and deeper the bond among those who experienced the event or tragedy together.

On April 6, 2018, a bus carrying twenty-eight members of the Humboldt Broncos Junior Hockey Team was on its way to a second-round playoff game in Saskatchewan, Canada, when a large transport truck did not stop as required at a highway intersection. The bus collided with the truck, killing ten players and six team staff. Of the twelve team members who survived, two were paralyzed and one suffered a traumatic brain injury that left him unable to speak or walk. The others suffered various serious injuries from which most have at least partially recovered.

In June 2021, more than three years after the tragedy, the surviving members of the team held a reunion for the first time since the accident. Ryan Straschnitzki, who remains paralyzed from the waist down, told a reporter, "We were a team before, but even closer now because of [the crash]. Because we all experienced it, in our own ways, but at the same time. We were all there, we were all involved in one way or another…. Knowing each other as the guys who survived the crash for the rest of our lives, it's something we didn't pick but it just happened."

Straschnitzki said he expected the friends and survivors to make the summertime reunion an annual event.[viii]

Social experiments

In our age of reality TV and the social experimentation that disguises itself as entertainment, a show called *The Island* featured a survival expert leading thirty men to a remote island, where he would drop them off to survive for thirty days. During this month-long period, participants went through many of the difficulties that survival scenarios typically create: finding water, preparing food, dealing with the injured, and of course, basic irritability caused by hunger and exhaustion. The primary theme of the show, clearly, was that the men suffered greatly.

In exit interviews, the men who made it through all thirty days described the profound bonding that took place during their suffering. Many of them reported how close they had grown to these other survivors and how they had never grown so close to anyone else in their entire lives. They bonded deeply with their fellow contestants in their month-long suffering, more deeply than ever before.

We see this phenomenon in much sharper relief through the connection of warriors after a combat deployment. All combat deployments can lead to life and death situations, miserable living conditions, and general suffering from day-in and day-out demands. When that intense suffering occurs while carrying out a significant mission, however, the bonds created among warriors tend to grow especially strong. One warrior described his experience of this phenomenon:

> "Being a part of a warrior tribe that has been through the fire together, you feel valued, you feel known, you have trust and you feel safe. Being ripped from that environment and not seeing it elsewhere is tough and it's traumatic. I mean, something beautiful dies in the process of that.
>
> "A big reason why a lot of people join the military is to find that brotherhood. To have that stripped from you and to see that it doesn't exist anywhere else—or it's hard to find—really tears you apart. A lot of places in the civilian world will give lip service to the suffering you went through. But they don't understand it because they don't have those past experiences (combat), they don't understand the world you're coming from. And even though you once were in the civilian world, when you're coming out of the military, it's hard to reset back to the civilian experience."

This warrior highlighted that the suffering of combat deepens the bond of the military brotherhood. When a warrior leaves the military, this sense of brotherhood is very difficult to replace, which emphasizes the power of suffering together.

Combat deployments often create the strongest and deepest bonds through the "fellowship of suffering," but the military

The suffering of combat deepens the bond of the military brotherhood. When a warrior leaves the military, this sense of brotherhood is very difficult to replace.

is adept at creating *many* opportunities for suffering. This typically begins at bootcamp, where most service members suffer more than they ever had up to that point in their lives. One Marine told me that his deployments to combat zones involved less suffering than what he had to endure during mountain warfare survival training, where he had to constantly fight off starvation and hypothermia.

Whenever warriors train for war, a great amount of suffering ensues. Leadership often uses that suffering to strengthen the mental toughness of their warriors, creating the expected result of unit bonding. Many warriors live by the mantra "more pain in peace, less blood in war." Leaders who adhere to this principle create opportunities for their unit to go through the pain together.

Any warrior who's been to the mountain warfare training center or the jungle warfare training center and other similar types of training environments will affirm that these places were created to induce suffering and pain. While the primary purpose of these training centers is to teach lessons that prove invaluable in severe environments, the secondary effect is having a unit suffer *together*. Many deep and lasting bonds are forged through suffering.

Not Months, But Years

Contrast the experience of reality TV contestants with military service members, who at minimum have suffered during basic training and through subsequent years (not months) of service. They have plenty of opportunities to bond!

Those who deploy to combat zones have more than enough opportunities to bond deeply, *much* more deeply than with others who have not shared with them the trauma of war. And again, it's not just the length of time they suffered together, or the depth of the losses they endured together, but that this suffering took place as they worked together to achieve some crucial mission aimed at saving the lives of many innocents.

Many warriors, after they get out and hold reunions with fellow veterans, whether formal or informal, spend their time reminiscing over their shared times of suffering. They typically incorporate humor as they recall together their experiences. As time passes, veterans often look back on their memories of suffering with fondness, usually after any trauma has been dealt with.

I once worked with a World War II veteran who landed as a medic on the beaches of Normandy, Omaha beach to be specific. We all know what that means. He had come in to see me after fifty-five years of stuffing his combat experience. He had finally reached mental breakdown status and decided to reach out for help.

After he worked through his trauma and some of the horrors he had experienced, he finally felt freed up to begin to see the significance of his service. He then began getting involved with World War II reunions and ceremonies, where he found bonding and healing. He eventually got on an honor flight and made it back to Normandy for the 75th anniversary. There he stood on the beaches and saluted all the men he had cared for and lost. He was there with other veterans who also had landed on Omaha beach, and though they did not know one another during their service, they knew one another because they had all suffered and bled together. Tears streamed down this veteran's face as he described his experience to me. The tears came not only from trauma, but out of gratitude and healing. I would highly recommend reading his story.[ix]

If you are a warrior, you already know this truth because you have experienced it. I could cite much research that corroborates the reality of the deep bonding that often takes place in combat zones or hazardous training environments, but warriors don't need such research to remind them of what they've personally experienced.

A Vietnam veteran described to me a powerful experience that illustrates this reality. He told me about an amazing leader who served as his direct officer. The vet was injured in battle and taken from the unit. For many years afterward, this officer would call him every October 14, along with all the other warriors under his command, to notify them how many men were still alive from their original unit. This continued to take place for fifty-three years post-Vietnam, when the officer died.

Think of that! The bond forged by their serving in combat together *for one year* kept them connecting for more than half a century. Not every unit does this, of course, but it illustrates that the experience of suffering together and trusting their lives to each other has such a potent impact that the connection can last for more than five decades.

A Powerful Warrior Identity

When you combine the personal warrior ethos, the communal warrior code, the clear and intense warrior purpose, and solidify all three with the warrior's suffering, the result is a powerfully significant and deeply ingrained warrior identity.

A great deal of intentional effort went into creating this identity and to make it so powerful. Please don't misconstrue this identity conditioning as something "bad"! In fact, it is one of the most powerful ways the military has of making our warriors into the best war fighters in the world. And not coincidentally, it's also one of the most effective ways we have of bringing our warriors back home alive.

The making of true warriors does not focus on making them into the most lethal fighters, but rather on transforming them into the very personification of great warriors. This process transforms their character to create warriors who know how to push themselves beyond normal capabilities and to sacrifice willingly for the sake of their country. Such a high order of conditioning can take ordinary civilians and transform them into tremendous, lethal war fighters.

But to make them into even *more* effective warriors, the conditioning doesn't stop there.

Pass and Review

- Suffering has a powerful bonding effect on the individuals who go through it together.
- Suffering acts as a potent catalyst to deeply instill the warrior identity.

Inspection

1. What level of suffering did you share with the warriors with whom you had the closest bond?

2. How well do you connect with others with whom you have not shared some experience of suffering? Does this ever become a problem? Explain.

8

★ ★ ★

Developmental Conditioning

We were at the age when we were begging for an identity.

The age of the recruit at the time of his or her initial conditioning is another powerful factor in the development of the warrior identity. The most common age of those going through basic training is eighteen to nineteen years old, a time in life that features some unique psychological characteristics.

Erikson's Theory of Development

Anyone who has taken a basic psychology class in college has learned about Erik Erikson's Theory of Development. Erikson's research concluded that several developmental milestones take place throughout one's life. Humans progress through multiple stages by the age of puberty, but somewhere around age twelve (or puberty), they enter adolescence. By this time, the major childhood developmental milestones have been reached, and then they enter into one of the more difficult stages: Identity versus role confusion. Erikson's theory says that adolescents either find an identity meaningful to them, or they struggle with role confusion.

What does this mean for potential warriors? The brains of the young civilians who sign up to join the military are still trying to figure out who they are. This biological and psychological phenomenon takes place just as these adolescents experience the potent mix of conditioning techniques used by the military. Just as this adolescent developmental timeframe solidifies, so does the conditioning and the modern-day rite-of-passage and a life-transforming experience. For these young warriors, role confusion is not the issue. Their warrior identity has become both clear and significant.

I often use an extended metaphor to explain this phenomenon to my veteran clients. Think of the development of adolescence like pouring concrete during childhood. You set up the frames into which you pour the concrete and then pour that concrete into those frames. The best time to work with concrete is not at the beginning, but when the concrete just begins to set. At that stage, it has solidified enough to hold the shapes that the frames dictate. At this point, you can make all the finishing touches you want and they become permanent.

> The suffering of combat deepens the bond of the military brotherhood. When a warrior leaves the military, this sense of brotherhood is very difficult to replace.

Late adolescence is like concrete just beginning to solidify. It is one of the best times to shape personal identity, just before that "concrete" sets. And, just like concrete, if you want to make changes to it after it sets, you can—but it'll take a jackhammer to do it.

This developmental timeframe is noteworthy because it emphasizes how young civilians entering the military, typically enlisted personnel, are in the developmental period precisely when their brains are searching for an identity they can hold onto. The military provides them a very powerful identity based on a warrior culture. The identity established by military conditioning is deeply ingrained in the warrior, not only because of personally held values, but also because of the developmental timeframe during which the value system is instilled.

Imagine that you take a conditioned warrior, long out of the identity development phase, and place him back into the civilian culture out of which he came. All the elements formerly in place to enhance and reinforce the warrior identity are gone. How well does the strong warrior identity now fit the civilian culture? The warrior's brain and body answered the question of personal identity years before and moved on. But veterans get suddenly thrust back into the challenge of trying to figure out who they are when they are no longer active war fighters—and they must do this work on their own.

We cannot downplay this point. It tremendously affects warriors of all ages who have begun making the transition back into the civilian world.

The "Nasty Civilians" Mentality

A significant aspect of the warrior identity instilled in us is the "nasty civilian" mentality. The military does *not* intentionally create in its soldiers ill will toward civilians, but this mentality naturally progresses within the warrior culture conditioning. It starts in boot camp.

At the beginning, recruits are made to feel less than civilians. As the transformation process continues, however, at some point they begin to feel superior to civilians. Drill instructors begin to emphasize this mentality in their language and references to civilians. Recruits frequently hear the phrase, "nasty civilians." The phrase means, of course, that civilians have not taken an oath to willingly sacrifice themselves for the benefit of the country, nor do they have a standard of conduct and honor that the warrior culture values. Inevitably, warriors begin to look down on the civilian culture.

Any civilian reading this should not feel alarmed. Such a mental shift is crucial as civilian recruits make the difficult transition to becoming warriors. As recruits begin to think of themselves as warriors, they prepare themselves for the big sacrifices they must make to benefit civilian culture.

Think of it this way. How do you get individuals to stand up and willingly sacrifice themselves for their peer group? Some do so because their unique character compels them to act for the benefit of others; but we all know that many warriors do not join the military for the sake of humanity. Some join because they see it as their only escape from a horrible personal situation. So, how does the military get these young citizens to place themselves at risk for the benefit of the greater populace? It all starts with how they view themselves.

We've already identified how most adults will naturally seek to protect young children. When researchers ask these adults why they would willingly put themselves in harm's way to protect children they don't even know; the most common answer is, "Because they cannot protect themselves." They might give the same answer in another way by replying, "Children are helpless. I am more capable than they are."

This very mindset is crucial for young warriors who must be trained to willingly move toward imminent danger or to put themselves in harm's way. They *must* believe and feel that they will put themselves in such harrowing places because those they protect cannot protect themselves. Such a powerful conviction transforms the civilian mindset into a warrior mindset. Most civilians will naturally move *away* from danger to preserve themselves, while warriors will immediately turn and move *toward* the threat. Warriors must develop such an automatic mindset if they are to effectively achieve their greater purpose.

I hope you see how important it is to create such a mindset in every warrior. But do you also see how this can create enormous difficulty for the warrior about to leave the military? How will he or she relate with civilians in a new workplace? How will these veterans develop friends in such a different social environment? How will they relate to new acquaintances and colleagues in the civilian world? Not every veteran has trouble in these areas, of course, but many do. Can you see how it could be a potential problem for all veterans?

To make a successful transition from military life to civilian life, some important mental shifts must take place. For many warriors, these shifts take years to occur, mostly because they have not grasped the enormous difference between the warrior mindset and the civilian mindset. When I ask them, "How many close friends do you have?" they will often reply, "very few," or even, "none"—other than those with whom they served in the military.

One former Army infantryman who had multiple combat tours deeply struggled in this area. This became such a struggle for him that as he went through college and even graduate school, he was not able to make friends with his peer group. He always had frustration with their mindsets and often lack of real-world experience. The academic environment did not help this area because they would often discuss global issues that were taking place and how many of the students would pontificate on what they felt was appropriate or the right thing to do. When he would add his two cents from experiencing different countries and cultures he would feel ostracized. In addition, because he was in school, he was unable to fully establish a new identity, so he held onto his past identity of being a combat infantryman, and you could see it proudly on the back of his vehicle with his large CIB (combat Infantry badge) decal for all to see. This became such a problem for him and his spouse because the spouse would often complain, "We don't go out and do anything, or have any friends that we hang out with." This veteran's reluctance to adapt into the civilian culture ultimately drove a wedge between him and his spouse. The spouse just wanted to do things and have a social life, but the veteran was unable to meet her needs in this. Unfortunately it led to the destruction of this marriage. But this is just one example of how the psychological transformation can impact the rest of a veteran's civilian life out of the military.

Identity Confusion or Crisis

The conditioning required to turn a civilian into a warrior has a tremendous impact on multiple levels of a warrior's physiology and psychology. Naturally, when a warrior leaves the environment that formed this identity, he or she will encounter some significant difficulties. The many mechanisms placed in the military setting to reinforce and remind warriors of their identity are now gone.

Once the active-duty service member becomes a veteran and no longer is inundated with environmental factors that reinforce the warrior identity, the consequences can have a tremendous impact. Those who lose their identity are like a ship without a sail, drifting wherever the ocean currents send them. This tremendously difficult transition for the warrior is rarely understood or even considered, despite the enormity of its impact.

Warriors who do not transition their identity become isolated. Because they insist on holding tight to their past identity, they refuse to allow themselves to interact or adapt to civilian environment. When you think of the developmental aspects we addressed, this lack of willingness makes more sense. Regardless of how much "sense" it makes, however, problems are sure to follow.

Another great divide occurs when a warrior tries to reconnect with a civilian peer group. The nature of the military experience has given warriors vastly different life experience from their civilian counterparts. This conditioning makes it difficult for many warriors to fit in with their old peer group (see Chapter 13). Or they may enter an academic environment where their new peer group is several years younger than they are. Veterans often complain that because their new peer group has not experienced greater parts of reality, they often make statements out of ignorance. As you can readily imagine, this can create issues.

When you are used to having leaders older than you, and you go to work for a boss younger than you—who lacks even a fraction of the life experience you have—problems can arise. Veterans might even take issue with professors whom they believe have not experienced "the greater realities of life." One combat veteran who served in the push to Iraq told me about his experiences with professors:

> "It drives me crazy that these professors will push their viewpoints down our throats and then, when we try and give our experiences outside of the United States as a reference point, they look at us like we are usurping their authority. These professors have done nothing but school and have very little life experience in the larger world, and now they are the ones who are dictating to me my future or saying my viewpoints are wrong?"

Unfortunate Results

When many veterans get out of the service, they begin searching for a new identity. The significant experiences that separate them from their civilian counterparts create strong barriers that they often find difficult to overcome by themselves. A host of consequences flow out from this this.

Many veterans still live and talk as if they were still in the military. When I work with veterans, we call this the "Uncle Rico Syndrome." One significant character in the movie *Napoleon Dynamite* is a man named Rico who has floundered in life ever since his "glory days" in high school football. Rico constantly tries to relive those glory days and continually asks himself, *What if?* His past identity haunts him and keeps him from finding a new one that would give him a chance to thrive. He struggles with his current pathetic identity as a mediocre Tupperware salesman.

Older generations might remember Al Bundy from the television show *Married with Children*. Al is a middle-aged man also struggling to hold onto his former identity as a high school football star. He despises his current life because it refuses to recognize or even remember his former identity. He has a job as an inept shoe salesman. Both Al and Rico long for the past, a revered time when they felt they lived the better part of themselves.

Many veterans resonate with Uncle Rico or Al Bundy because their past identity as warriors remains stronger than their present identity as citizens. As a result, many put stickers on the back of their cars or wear military paraphernalia that identifies them as a former service member.

This does not suggest that getting recognition for one's service to the country is a bad thing! Veterans simply look to this area as a reminder of a strong, past identity.

When someone tries to live out a former identity today, however, the attempt leads to continuous frustration, disappointment, and even depression. Such an exercise has neither a present nor a future. To say it another way, men and women in this predicament believe the best part of themselves is behind them. If the best lies in the past, however, then they have very little to look forward to. And that depresses them.

> When someone tries to live out a former identity today, the attempt leads to continuous frustration, disappointment, and even depression. Such an exercise has neither a present nor a future.

Derek Weida, a former Army paratrooper who lost his leg in Iraq, told a TV interviewer about his difficulties in transitioning back into the civilian world: "I thought that being a soldier was all I had to offer this world." He then explained how his struggle through rehabilitation led to significant levels of depression, in large part because he did not know what he would be after he could no longer be a soldier. His depression grew so severe that he became suicidal—and he insisted, "it was not PTSD." Once his identity as a soldier disappeared, he had only loss to fill the void. His despair over losing his purpose as a soldier exaggerated his loss.

A former Army infantry officer who had successfully led his men in combat through multiple deployments to Iraq struggled to get on his feet after he left the service. An unfortunate event in which he was wrongly arrested and thrown in jail caused him to fixate on this injustice, especially because of how he had served his country. His fixation festered and fed his anger to the point where he could not keep a job. He got released from several jobs because of his general irritability. He would always tell himself, "They don't know what I've done for this country." He eventually became homeless and could not move forward. His identity got stuck in his warrior persona and the injustices he suffered only solidified his "stuckness," becoming a slippery slope that led to deeper and deeper depression.

Treatment for PTSD will not solve this warrior's problems. He must be helped to find a new identity, one that borrows helpfully from his former warrior identity.

A Soldier Without a Country

Some warriors do not live in the past but instead jettison all they received from their military experience the moment they get out. They have a complete aversion to everything about their military service—and they, too, struggle with making the transition.

I've worked with many veterans over the years who just want to move past their warrior season of life. Their problem is that, by doing so, they also lose many valuable skill sets. The decision to ignore their military history often begins a desperate search for both a new personal identity and a new culture with which they can identify. Many veterans subsequently begin to identify themselves with things far too small to adequately replace their warrior experience.

I once worked with a veteran who had only one goal: to work as a stock trader on Wall Street and become a millionaire. The military had processed him out of the service after he suffered an injury that prevented him from fulfilling his assigned role. He walked with shame and wanted to find *anything* to replace that ingrained military identity. Going from a life of service to a life of selfish pursuit, however, left him both empty and void.

Whenever you try to replace a very strong identity with something far less potent, an internal void ensues. If you have a strong identity built on sound morals and values, but then try to replace it with a more selfish identity, you will have problems. I do not mean that a banker making millions of dollars has a weaker identity than a warrior, but a warrior who tries to exchange his service mentality for a more self-aggrandizing perspective will soon feel a loss of both significance and honor. It's almost inevitable.

A Questionable Future

The future is another area that can be problematic for a once powerful warrior. Warriors who lack an identity or culture to bolster and direct their current situation will struggle to find direction and purpose for their lives. I have worked with scores of veterans who deeply struggled to figure out what their future should look like. I've also seen veterans who choose a new direction immediately after they leave active duty, only to find that it leaves them wanting *more*.

> "Warriors who lack an identity or culture to bolster and direct their current situation will struggle to find direction and purpose for their lives.

If you were active in a vocation that constantly makes use of your identity, would you feel more fulfilled than if you did something always outside of your identity? The question points to the enormous difficulty for veterans. They come from a place where identity and purpose were clear and deeply intertwined. Their future typically pointed to a greater mission and purpose.

Once out of the military, however, they must direct their own future and determine their own purpose. Unfortunately, many fail to do this and flounder in the civilian world, not because of a lack of capability, but because they have not adapted their warrior identity to directly correspond to a successful future in the civilian world.

When we try to live without a meaningful current identity, we begin a slow slide into despair. A lack of identity is a problem for all men, but those who have gone from a very strong identity to a former or abandoned identity will feel a sense of hopelessness and confusion. Add these personal components to the larger components of cultural influences and you get a perfect storm. For many of us, this storm can become the greatest we have ever had to face, because we no longer have the same support that we once did. And much of the civilian support that does surround us either does not fully understand the real issue or tries to make it about something that it isn't. I have worked with many combat veterans who would rather go back to combat rather than squarely face this reality.

A Final Complicating Factor

Are you beginning to see both the complexity and the far-reaching nature of the urgent transition problem facing most veterans? Incredibly, we have yet more to explore in trying to understand the full scope of what goes into making a warrior—and why transitioning back to civilian life poses such a challenge.

No inquiry into this issue could be considered complete without delving into the cultural conditioning that all warriors undergo. It, too, plays a significant role in the transformation process of citizens into warriors, and therefore adds yet another complicating factor to any successful transition.

Pass and Review

- A young service member during his or her development period is searching for identity and purpose.
- The typical developmental timeframe is usually closed for most warriors after their years of service.
- Warriors need to feel that they are superior to their civilian counterparts so that they have more of a compulsion to protect them.
- Warriors leaving the military typically find it very difficult to change their deeply instilled identity, which means the process of transition can get stuck.
- Living out a past identity when it is not currently active can create a recipe for depression.

Inspection

1. What made you join the military?
2. How receptive were you to conditioning when you joined the military? How open and willing were you to receive the warrior identity?
3. Do you see yourself as superior to the civilian? Explain.
4. Who are you, once you are no longer an active-duty warrior?

9

★ ★ ★

Cultural Conditioning

The culture of the military is a primary personal influencer.

We now shift to the final area of influence we will consider that goes into making a warrior. All these areas overlap and impact every other area. I separate them only to help us better understand the depth and the details of how the military conditions a civilian to become a war fighter.

Veterans quickly recognize this final area, especially when they comment on their loss of camaraderie (as they often do). I lecture at a college class called "boots to books" for veterans who have begun to attend college. I always ask my students to name the most difficult things about leaving active duty. They typically agree on two: the loss of close friendships and feeling that they don't fit in. One Infantry Marine told me, "I feel like my culture was completely torn away from me. It was done. Superman suit got hung up and it was back to just being Joe Schmoe. It blew my mind. I was in culture shock to the max."[xi]

> I feel like my culture was completely torn away from me. It was done. Superman suit got hung up and it was back to just being Joe Schmoe. It blew my mind. I was in culture shock to the max." — A former infantry Marine

I have heard the same sentiment expressed to me countless times over the years. Both issues revolve around the final area of the warrior's conditioning.

Social and Economic Conditioning

I became aware of this area after I left the Marines and took a sociology class in which we learned about world cultures. As the instructor displayed on a screen the elements that differentiate a primary culture from a sub-culture, I had an epiphany.

The warrior culture meets many of the criteria for a primary culture, I realized. The conclusion shocked me. Consider some of the criteria that define a primary culture. Primary cultures have several practices and standards in common, including:

- *Social Organization:* Distinct family roles and rules for engaging in relationships
- *Customs and Traditions:* Rules for behavior and celebrations
- *Religion:* Answers to the basic questions of life
- *Language:* Distinct vocabulary, syntax, and idioms, including dialects and jargon
- *Arts, Literature, and Education:* Public expressions of cultural values
- *Form of Government:* Clear structure of established legal systems and who holds power
- *Economic System:* How a group uses resources and land to meet communal needs

The warrior culture replicates many of these areas, often differing in substantial ways from the civilian culture that it serves. Let's look in more detail at each area.

Social Organization

It does not naturally occur to us that the military has a distinctly different social organization than the civilian world. Yet it becomes easy to see the clash of cultures whenever the two worlds begin to interact.

1. Mission before family

While family provides the basic social organization of the military, things look quite different there than they do in the civilian world. My years of working with active-duty couples have taught me that these couples must address a major issue. Whoever the service member is, the spouse must come to understand that the mission of the unit comes before the family. The sooner spouses accept this reality, the better they can deal with the frustrations that come because of it. The fact that mission comes before family increases the divorce rate for all service members, but for female service members, the rate is even higher.

Civilians often say that family comes first and that individuals should base their career and life decisions on that life priority. Those who enter the military and swear to a code, however, give up the family as their top priority. Their top priority becomes mission.

I have known myriad military families in which a child is born a few weeks after a deployment, but the service member remains on deployment or must still leave for a training exercise. At times, of course, commands make certain accommodations for unusual cases, but when the warrior does not *want* to sacrifice the mission for the sake of family, it can cause irreparable relationship wounds. Military spouses must learn to embrace this "mission first" reality and how to deal with regular moves and new duty stations.

2. Strong non-family bonds

Military service members also tend to make strong bonds with their fellow warriors. I have worked with many couples who have struggled because the warrior makes significant life decisions based on deep friendships made with other warriors.

One couple made an appointment to see me after the warrior had been unfaithful to his partner while on deployment. After he returned, he honestly admitted his adultery and was truly contrite about his behavior. As this couple worked to repair their relationship, a fellow warrior asked the military husband to attend his wedding, as well as the night-before bachelor party, which would include the wild festivities commonly associated with such celebrations. In the civilian world, where the family takes priority and precedence, the bachelor party likely would have been a big "no-go." But because the service member had deployed to combat zones with the groom-to-be, he refused to say no. The couple found this decision very difficult to work through. It's a common challenge unique to a military environment.

The bonds of military service, especially when solidified through combat, grow to a deep level usually followed by a deep sense of loyalty. Many service members feel closer to their warrior friends than they do to immediate family. Their treatment of both reflects this perspective.

3. Segregation of authority

At some level, all branches of military service segregate officers from enlisted personnel, although some services take this to more of an extreme than others. Most military services separate the officer quarters from the enlisted quarters. Quite often they separate the officers' club and the enlisted club, a division that can extend to the mess hall, where you may find an officers' section and an enlisted section.

In the Marine Corps and in many other services, the Uniform Code of Military Justice prohibits fraternization and provides punishments for violators. This applies particularly to inappropriate relationships between an officer or senior enlisted with a subordinate or someone of lower rank. Those of us who have lived in a military culture completely understand the reason for this strict segregation. In the warrior culture, authority and the protection of authority are vital to the effective functioning of a unit.

Many more examples could be cited that illustrate the different social roles common in the military. These roles usually differ from those of our culture of origin, yet for military personnel they make sense (most of the time).

Customs and Traditions

Anyone who has lived in a military environment knows the clear distinction in customs and traditions between the warrior culture and the civilian world. It is part of what makes the warrior culture so unique.

Customs and traditions vary. Some Army cavalry units, for example, have significant traditional indoctrinations that must take place before a warrior can earn "spurs" to put on a uniform. In such units, warriors do not feel a part of the culture until they earn their "spurs." Such practices play out in various ways with different units, but all of them rely on tradition, custom, and heritage to build a member's sense of personal identity.

Every culture has unique traditions and customs that are primary to it. The warrior culture, for example, has many celebratory practices that don't exist in the civilian world. Most military services celebrate their service inception date ("birthday") with some community celebration, much as civilians would celebrate the Fourth of July. The warrior culture, however, infuses its celebrations with a deep sense of reverence. Many veterans come in to see me, frustrated with civilian holidays such as Veterans Day and Memorial Day. "They don't truly honor the meaning of these holidays," these veterans complain.

Military traditions and celebrations bring to focus why so many of us and our friends sacrifice our own personal freedoms. Our traditions bring deep meaning to our celebrations and to our lives. Active-duty Marines celebrate the Marine Corps birthday every year. When many Marines leave the military, they continue to celebrate the birthday of the Corps. Such a practice helps them to retain at least a part of the warrior culture they once lived in, and to keep alive their warrior identity long after they have separated from active-duty life.

Other less significant customs and traditions also affect a warrior's daily life. Consider the tradition of morning and evening colors, when the U.S. flag is raised and lowered on a flagpole. This practice takes place twice a day, followed with a bugle call sent over the entire base. When the bugle call goes out for "colors," all military personnel stop whatever they are doing. If outside, they face the flagpole and salute for the entire colors bugle call. The tradition lasts especially long on Sunday because whatever service branches are stationed at that base play their hymns as a formal way to honor the flag and the purpose for which the warrior culture exists. Warriors stop everything in their day to remember the reason behind what they do. This powerful tradition has become increasingly rare in the civilian world.

Remember the tradition that forbids Marines from walking on the grass in military installations? Although no one knows why the tradition started, it has been carried on throughout the generations. One salty warrior told me that the tradition comes from a time when minefields were prominent. The prohibition was designed to condition warriors to avoid certain areas, even if it shortened the route to their objective. Sounds reasonable to me. It also reminds me of another tradition in which we were conditioned to walk in the chow hall with our hand on top of an open cup and shout, "gang way, live grenade!" Either way, the tradition became ingrained into our behavior.

Traditions like these (and countless more) help warriors to identify with their military culture and separate it from the civilian culture. Customs and traditions become a significant factor separating one culture from the other. More to the point of this book, to leave a culture rich in such tradition and to enter a culture that more heartily celebrates change and innovation can feel like boarding a ship that lacks an anchor.

> "To leave a culture rich in tradition and to enter a culture that more heartily celebrates change and innovation can feel like boarding a ship that lacks an anchor.

Spirituality and Religion

The warrior culture accepts diversity in the practice of faith. Still, the warrior culture usually has a single entity, a chaplain, there to minister to warriors regardless of their faith practice. All chaplains know and accept that their primary purpose in the military is to serve and protect their country. Their role is to minister to all warriors who have chosen to take the oath.

Chaplains serve directly under the commanding officer of the unit to which they minister. It's a unique role in the military, particularly because of the U.S. practice of separation of church and state. The military continues this practice, despite the political difficulties it can create in the civilian world. The military brings these worlds together for the overarching purpose of aiding the warrior mission. The mission and our duty to it create a unique form of faith practice in the military.

One Army chaplain deployed to Afghanistan with the 101st airborne. Along with his theological studies, he had majored in film. He learned that if he was to be a good chaplain to his men—who had varying practices of faith—he would need to go out on patrol with them. "I couldn't carry a weapon as a chaplain," he said, "so I carried a camera." He filmed even during fire fights, stating, "even though these guys don't practice the same faith as me, my job is still to minister to them."

The point is that the military culture has a distinct faith practice separate from the civilian culture. Those of us who have experienced it can agree that it differs markedly from the religious practice we experience in civilian life.

Language

The military culture uses the English language in a starkly different way than what one typically finds in the civilian world. Veterans often get blank looks from non-military types when these former warriors use language commonly used in the service, such as, "Oscar Mike, ETA five mikes." Those words make no sense to someone who's never been part of the military culture. (The quoted words mean, "On my way, be there in five minutes.")

Observers who attend military events often feel confused by the unique dialect and jargon used among warriors. What confuses civilians about this military language? It's similar to the misunderstandings that often happen when traveling internationally.

Travelers sometimes get a shock when they visit a foreign country where the citizens there speak the same language as the traveler, and yet miscommunication abounds. Different dialects produced by differing primary cultures can make the same primary language sound almost like a different tongue. Any American who has visited England or Australia understands that unique dialects of the same language sometimes make conversation nearly impossible. The English of one group sounds unintelligible to the other. Different phrases, slang, jargon, alternate spellings of words, accents, and diverse pronunciations can combine to create rampant miscommunication.

Military personnel speak an almost cryptic form of English. If I were to label it, I might call it, "Acronymic English." The military *constantly* uses acronyms to condense long, descriptive terms. Already in this book you've seen acronyms such as MOS, UCMJ, MEPS, UA, NJP, PTSD. Acronyms proliferate in the military like rabbits.

When I was in the Marines, I often played a popular boardgame called Taboo. Teams try to guess a target word without using a list of forbidden words. Civilians quickly made it clear that military personnel could not play on the same team, because they would use their unique military dialect to describe the target word without using the forbidden terms. We all spoke English, but warriors could use a dialect unintelligible to civilians.

The warrior culture has a distinct dialect and terminology of its own that distinguishes its use of the English language from the primary civilian culture American English. And that, too, can cause problems for the warrior transitioning out of the military and into the civilian world.

Arts, Literature, and Education

The warrior culture expresses itself in arts and literature differently than does the civilian culture. While the warrior culture still enjoys music created by the civilian culture, just as foreign cultures enjoy American music, the arts and literature that truly express the warrior culture look distinctly different.

Some unique forms of artistic expression take place on military installations. The Marine Corps is known for painting rocks and other inanimate objects red and yellow to represent the Corps' colors. Other military services use their own branch's colors to do the same thing.

Unit insignias have a distinct meaning and expression of power to everyone who has ever served in that unit. The unit/crest or insignia, something like a modern-day coat of arms, represents a unique battle history that makes up part of the personal identity adopted by the warrior. Warriors typically take great personal pride in their unit emblems. If you drive on a military installation, you will see military crests all over the place, each of them identifying specific units. Something similar happens in civilian culture when college graduates wear with great pride the colors and symbols of their university or college. The major difference is that most warriors are willing to fight and die to represent their unit's crest.

The unit crest has a distinctly powerful influence on a warrior. Although the crest is "merely" an artistic expression of the battle legacy of a unit, it holds deep meaning and sparks a deep commitment for which the warrior is willing to bleed. Civilians will not recognize what the crest means or what it represents, but to the warrior, that crest carries a tremendous amount of personal significance.

Education norms also can look very different in warrior culture than in civilian culture. The military often condenses the timeframe in which a warrior must learn some given content. Military schools commonly take a normal semester's worth of content and cram it into several short weeks, cutting the normal classroom time in half and using the rest of the time for "practical application." Instructors want warriors to get out of the classroom and apply their new skills or knowledge. Final tests include both academic/classroom learning as well as evaluation of lesson application.

Veterans who go to college often struggle with academics, at least initially. They often complain that they get only classroom time and not practical application time. Many warriors found out how to learn using the instruction/application format, and when colleges don't use this format, veterans often feel frustrated and have trouble retaining what they've learned. Fortunately, many colleges and universities now accept for credit coursework completed in military schools.

Form of Government

Recruits quickly learn that the military is not a democracy. Ironically, in order to preserve the democracy of larger civilian culture, an authoritarian form of government in the military is required. That military government more closely resembles a monarchy.

One person at the top is in charge, disseminating commands that must be followed unquestioningly by the whole. It is often said, "It takes a dictatorship to protect a democracy."

Military government looks different not only because of who is in charge, but also because the warrior culture lives by entirely different codes, as we've seen. This code is legally enforceable through the Uniform Code of Military Justice. The UCMJ differs completely from the civilian legal system and often enforces its laws in different ways.

A battalion commander, for example, can become both judge and jury for a warrior accused of violating the UCMJ. The commander can take a service member who has committed a minor offense—not a court-martial offense—and reduce or remove his rank or reduce his pay for some indeterminate period. He can also curtail his freedom by keeping him on barracks restriction for a certain amount of time. Can you imagine in the civilian world having a boss who could demote you, dock your pay, and restrict you to your home for up to ninety days? Can you imagine being required to check in with your work every hour, in your uniform? We can only imagine the lawsuits that would follow.

The warrior culture also has its own police force and is sovereign over its own land. Very few people groups in the United States have sovereignty of their own land and their own law enforcement organizations to enforce their unique culture's laws. The closest examples are Native American tribes who enforce their own laws through their own law enforcement entities. The United States military also has sovereignty over its land, separate from state jurisdictions, as well as its own police force to enforce its own laws.

Economic System

Military culture has a different economic system than civilian culture. Even though both use the same currency, the way warriors get that currency differs markedly from their civilian counterparts.

Military personnel do not get paid by the hour. I once heard Marines talking about how much they made. When they averaged the number of hours they worked and their total pay in a year, they concluded that they earned about $.70 an hour. It can surprise you to hear what military service members talk about as they sit in a bunker, waiting for time to pass!

Military culture also differs from civilian culture because it does not depend on supply and demand. Whatever warriors need to complete their mission, the military provides. While military personnel rarely get *all* they need to complete a mission, the principle remains the same.

This form of economic system has some distinct benefits. It can, for example, create great security for family members and spouses. Warriors know they will get a paycheck on the first and fifteenth of the month, like clockwork (except for periodic government shutdowns).

An Existential Birth

The warrior culture meets almost all the criteria for a primary culture, except for one element that causes some to challenge the idea. The challengers say, "But no one is born into it." These critics contend that unless a culture gets passed down through heredity and genetics, it cannot be a primary culture.

I would reply that while no warrior is born into the culture genetically, they most certainly are born into it existentially. That is, no one gets to just walk in and become part of the military culture. It takes time, training, and willing participation in certain rites of passage to become part of the military culture. In fact, the warrior culture meets more of the criteria for a primary culture than it does for a subculture.

Why have I taken so much space to explain this issue? It's critical to understand that when a recruit enters the warrior culture, he or she is *completely* surrounded by a primary culture, with all the distinctives that this implies. It's much like getting taken to a foreign country, dropped into a unique culture, having to learn a dialect of English different than your own, and immersed in practices radically different from the ones you have known since childhood.

When a veteran leaves a warrior culture to enter a civilian culture, there *will* be some culture shock. Even warriors sometimes downplay this transition because they think, *I came from this culture so it will be no big deal to return to it.* The problem they don't consider is that warriors have come to see military culture as the highest form of culture. Returning to the civilian world is often considered a *big* step down.

From Conditioning to Challenge

I designed Part One of this book to help you better understand the conditioning that goes into making civilians into war fighters. While insight can be helpful, we also need to look at how these areas can create problems. If you are better aware of the problems that you are facing and where they are coming from, you will be able to better navigate them.

A good place to start may be to ask why most veterans think of civilian culture as "less than" military culture. It may help to consider the primary values of the warrior culture, which greatly affect the way a warrior returns to the civilian world.

Pass and Review

- The warrior culture meets many of the criteria for a primary culture.
- The warrior culture has unique social standards and expectations for its warriors and their families.

- The warrior culture has its own distinct traditions and practices that are very different than the civilian culture.
- The warrior culture has its own practice and acceptance of faith.
- The warrior culture has a unique dialect of English that is almost unintelligible for the outsider.
- The warrior culture has different forms artistic forms of expression, and a very different method of educating their people.
- The military is not a democracy, we give that up to defend the democracy.
- Every warrior has to be "born" into the culture.

Inspection

1. Name several of the biggest cultural differences you see between the warrior culture and the civilian culture.
2. Do you see the military as a primary culture? Explain.

★ ★ ★

PART TWO

The Warrior's Challenge

10

★ ★ ★

Culture Shock and Displacement

The culture shock surprises many as they return to the civilian world.
You don't simply walk back in as if nothing happened since you left.

Since the warrior culture is more of a primary culture than a secondary one, leaving it gives most warriors culture shock. Their experience closely resembles what happens when an immigrant from a foreign nation and culture moves to the United States. While some immigrants quickly adapt to the new culture, many others struggle to make the transition and so try to create their own microcosm of their former culture in their new environment.

While I do not believe it's "wrong" or "bad" to hold on to some aspects of a former culture that one knew and loved, problems inevitably arise when immigrants refuse to adapt to the other culture and instead try to re-create their former culture in their new living environment. An isolated community usually results that does not interact well with the indigenous culture. This lack of adaptation naturally creates barriers that typically produce serious consequences.

The same phenomenon can take place among warriors. When they reject civilian culture but fail to find any pocket of culture with which they can align themselves, they

> When warriors reject civilian culture but fail to find any pocket of culture with which they can align themselves, they end up choosing isolation. And an isolated individual is clearly asking for trouble . . . big trouble.

end up choosing isolation. And an isolated individual is clearly asking for trouble ... *big* trouble.

Since all cultures develop norms that influence the common aspects of life, let's identify a few key values of the warrior culture. Many of them you are aware of, but for clarity, let's describe them.

A Performance-Based Culture

Perhaps the most dominant aspect of the warrior culture is its basis in performance. Parents of teenagers whose children want to join the Marine Corps often ask me to discuss with their kids what they're about to get into. I always tell them to remember that they are entering a performance-based culture.

"Your performance will impact every aspect of your experience," I typically say. "If you are not fitting in, the only way to get better acceptance is to perform your duties at a higher level."

This only makes sense when you consider that mission accomplishment is the primary value of the culture you want to join. In the work arena, there is no quicker way to find yourself rejected than by failing to perform. In the military, non-performance can lead to catastrophe.

A culture that values performance because of the extreme nature of the task it must accomplish will overlook classic discriminating factors or cultural taboos that otherwise might get somebody ostracized. Such a culture will tend to accept anyone with physical prowess who competently performs an assigned mission task. This does not mean that everyone in the culture will want to hang out with the person during times of liberty, but that person will be accepted as part of the group.

The warrior culture has individuals of completely different cultural backgrounds, who normally would never spend time together, who now work together for untold numbers of hours, days, weeks, months, even years. That's unique.

While in the school of infantry, I spent time with a Hispanic male who was into techno music and the rave scene. I was a country boy from Utah who could think of nothing further from my experience. I found myself spending a lot of time with this inner-city kid whose music preferences completely differed from my own. We felt drawn together because we both had a drive to excel in our given MOS. That singular desire bridged our gap of civilian cultural differences. We both had a strong drive to perform.

Of course, a performance-based culture also comes with negative side effects. The opposite of performance is failure/shame. In the warrior culture, we always said we had three ways to get people to conform to standards: pain, shame, and paperwork—and nobody wants to do paperwork.

We will revisit this topic of performance and shame in the next chapter, but for now, it's important to understand that when somebody in a warrior culture fails to perform to some known standard, pain, and/or shame always follow. Usually it is both, because such an unpleasant mixture motivates people to move more quickly toward the standard.

Consider, then, what often happens when a warrior transitions from a military culture with clear standards of performance to a civilian culture where the standards seem murky at best. Culture shock typically results, often accompanied by anger and confusion.

Let me give two examples. The first has to do with your vocation. One former combat engineer Marine experienced the frustration of unclear standards of his new workplace as a civilian. He got out of the Marine Corps and diligently worked through the process to become an electrical engineer. After completing his schooling, he got a job doing engineering entry-level jobs, which were usually mundane tasks of inspecting parts. After only months in this new job, he would come into counseling with complaints and frustration on how he felt that his employers had thrown him into production requirements without giving him clear training or clear standards of how he needs to perform. He would complain that his supervisor would just come to him in frustration from the production expectations he had (which were not clearly communicated), and then make demands that things needed to be produced at a greater level. With the military mindset of commitment to mission, he would stay late and complete tasks only to the detriment of his own well-being. He eventually had to leave this job because of the stress and pressure due to this frustration. He came from a culture in which the standards of performance were clear. He fell into the trap of his new employers expecting an outcome, but in the military mindset, not giving the proper training to equip for that type of production. This was a significant culture shock for the veteran as he tried to assimilate to the civilian world.

The second example has to do with the standards of being a husband or wife, and father or mother. Once you've left the military, and the dominant area of your life that was holding you to standards is gone, you begin to measure yourself off of the relationships around you. Your marriage and your parenting are often places that a veteran begins to seek standards. In the vacuum of the loss of military performance standards we begin to construct pseudo standards. However, this can be very frustrating because of the lack of clarity and standards when it comes to being a good partner in marriage or being a good parent. If anything the standards are absolutely not clear. If anything, warriors can be guilty of enforcing rigid standards in their attempt to create a similar structure for performance, which only leads to greater frustration within the family and marriage. I so often hear the complaint from family members of warriors, "We did not join the military, but you were treating us as if we were your subordinates." Now, when the warrior starts hearing these things from his family it is usually due the warrior trying to apply the standards that he learned in the military to another domain of life. Which does not always work well because the focus of the military is mission, the focus of the marriage and family is relationship.

In both of these examples I am trying to show common consequences of the performance culture. When they are not adapted, they create frustration for all the parties involved.

An Honor/Respect-Based Culture

The military culture is based on honor and respect. While those values get applied in multiple ways, rank structure tends to dominate.

Through the rank structure, honor and respect receive their structure and status. This is expressed primarily through symbolic gestures such as saluting those of a higher rank and referencing the rank before one's title. If you're talking to a superior enlisted servicemember, for example, you speak the person's rank before the last name. It would be considered an insult if you just called him by his last name. If you pass an officer without saluting, this form of disrespect could be punished. The warrior culture has multiple, daily forms of respect built into it.

Noteworthy accomplishments also are respected and achievable by all ranks. One's uniform displays one's accomplishments. The medals and ribbons a warrior can earn provide a form of a respect in an honor-based culture. When warriors look at those ribbons, they search for the ones that demand their respect. One of the most classic ones features a combat "V" on a personal award. A baby blue ribbon demands respect as it holds the medal of honor, our highest award for valor and gallantry. Even the civilian culture gives respect to this type of award. Various medals and ribbons announce the basics of an honor and respect-based culture.

Culture shock in this area sometimes confuses people. How can coming from an honor and respect-based culture create culture shock upon re-entering the civilian world? In one way, it can come from not knowing your place and where you stand in the pecking order. Many warriors struggle with the regular disrespect they see among the civilian populace. Warriors may struggle when they see a subordinate show disrespect to a boss or refuse to comply with a superior. It can get even worse if *they* are the superior in the workplace being disrespected by some subordinate.

In the warrior culture, even if you did not personally respect the person, you respected his or her rank and had to follow his or her orders. What a different scenario in the civilian world! Veterans can have high sensitivity to being disrespected in the civilian culture. Because the warrior culture has many clear protocols regarding the respect shown to those of higher rank, entering a civilian world that lacks these protocols can cause the warrior to feel disrespected. One of the most common complaints I have heard from veterans throughout the years is the way they feel disrespected in their daily on-the-job interactions.

A Pride-Based Culture

Many individuals feel attracted to the military by observing those in the military. They notice a sense of confidence and strength exuded by trained warriors that creates in the observers a sense of cultural pride.

In the military, pride pushes those who would not normally push themselves. I am not talking about the abusive pride that reveals itself as arrogance, although this does occur in the military. I have in mind the sense of high self-worth and value. This kind of pride is instilled in the warrior. Warriors know they will be held to a higher standard.

The members of a pride-based culture have a deep unwillingness to be viewed as injured or hurt. Warriors commonly ignore injuries or disregard embarrassment because they do not wish to look weak. This culture has a revulsion toward weakness because pride drives the ego. It's rightly said that the warrior culture is an alpha dog environment in which continuous fighting goes on to see who is on top. The rank structure of the military limits this kind of fighting, but high competition always exists among individual warriors. With this high competition comes an aversion for embarrassment and any display of weakness.

From boot camp on, alphas prey on the weak mentality and seek to extinguish it. Anyone in boot camp showing any form of weakness will soon find themselves surrounded by drill instructors, like sharks picking up the scent of blood in the water. They jump on any display of weakness. I once heard a Marine say that he became emotionally overwhelmed when he felt he had disappointed himself and his drill instructors. When water began to leak from his eyes, the drill instructors pounced on him in an upbraiding and vicious way. In the civilian world, of course, this would be termed bullying. In the warrior culture, this is considered conditioning, because such weakness negatively affects the warrior's ability to perform and so puts units at risk.

Of course, such a pride-based culture has consequences. For one thing, a pride-based culture instills a sense of embarrassment in warriors who need to reach out for help. The barometer for evaluating what qualifies as weakness and what is a genuine need becomes skewed. When warriors leave the military and start to struggle in the civilian world, they usually have great difficulty in reaching out for help.

> It is a well-known fact that seven out of ten veteran suicides occur when veterans do not reach out for help and are not in the Veterans Administration system.

It is a well-known fact that seven out of ten veteran suicides occur when veterans do not reach out for help and are not in the Veterans Administration system. While many factors keep them from reaching out for help, the pride-based warrior culture and its aversion to feeling weak prompt many veterans to keep quiet about their struggles. Many veterans remember that when they were active duty, they were the ones demeaning anyone who reached out for help.

This emphasis on pride and aversion to showing weakness does not typically become catastrophic while the individual functions inside the warrior culture, because that culture keeps it in check. In the culture, the proximity and closeness of other warriors will force somebody to get help, especially if it affects the warrior's performance. Every warrior's performance affects the team; a lack of team cohesion affects operational readiness, and a lack of operational readiness means people will die.

Once a warrior leaves the military culture, however, all these parameters that keep pride-based problems in check go away. Struggling veterans who don't get the help they need tend to isolate themselves, which leads to depression, which leads to hopelessness, which too often leads to "fixing" the problem by suicide.

A Purpose-Based Culture

Military *service* implies that those in the military sought to connect with something bigger than themselves, to participate in some praiseworthy endeavor designed to benefit others. Anyone who enters the warrior culture is instilled with the idea that they are now part of a bigger unit with a bigger overall purpose. Ultimately, this purpose is the protection and security of the United States of America. Other levels of purpose follow.

Every job in the warrior culture is driven by a purpose derived from the primary purpose of serving the nation. Every occupation in the armed services has a specific military occupational specialty (MOS). Many warriors do not realize how much of an impact that MOS has on their personal identification. Each MOS has a specific mission and job title. The mission and job title spell out the specific way they get involved in the bigger purpose.

I sometimes ask infantry Marines, "What is the mission of the Marine Corps rifle squad?"

"To locate, close with, and destroy the enemy with fire and maneuver. And to repel enemies' assault with fire and close combat," they answer automatically. This answer describes the purpose of an infantry Marine. Each MOS has a specific purpose.

Many warriors feel frustrated, not because they did not have a purpose, but because they did not believe they were being used according to their purpose. This happens quite often, especially in times of war where the fluidity and changing nature of the current needs drive the use of the individual warrior.

Moreover, warriors who never actually went to war often feel that they did not fulfill their purpose. They have a sense of something missing, or even a sense of shame that they did not get the opportunity to complete their purpose. Civilians may see this conclusion as quite odd, but the warrior culture is a culture of purpose. When warriors do not believe that they have fulfilled that purpose, they often feel a powerful sense of shame.

A loss of purpose in civilian life can depress many veterans because, while on active duty the military, they had been part of a significant purpose. If somebody has never been part of something bigger than themselves and so never had a greater purpose, they simply don't know what they are missing. Warriors do not have that luxury because they *have* been part of a bigger purpose. When they move into the civilian arena, they become acutely aware of their loss of purpose.

I've seen warriors try to fill this loss of purpose with many things, but most of them never approach the same level of purpose they felt they had in the military. Because this issue has lingering effects on the warrior, we will address it in more detail in Chapter 12. How the warrior handles the issue can make his or her transition either significantly more difficult or significantly more meaningful.

A Code-Based Culture

We already discussed the Uniform Code of Military Justice (UCMJ) as a communal code enforced by the warrior culture. But the UCMJ is just one way the military expresses itself as a code-based culture.

In fact, the code and standard by which the warrior culture operates can look very different than the UCMJ. The UCMJ is merely the formal legal and civil law that keeps the military world in order. We've also seen how the military's many creeds also instill additional codes in their warriors.

This code-based culture has a standard for most things. It always tries to standardize the optimal performance it expects from its warriors. Layer upon layer of standards is therefore instilled into the codes of the warrior culture.

Specific units instill their own codes pertaining to their specific roles or missions. Basic codes can be instilled, such as the standard of "integrity." The military community can significantly punish a lack of integrity, even though the infraction may have no specific, formal, or legal basis. The warrior culture does not require formal, legal intervention to enforce a consequence. Unit commanders have the authority to enforce consequences that can significantly affect a warrior's life. Even small unit leaders can bring significant consequences to those who they believe are not adhering to the code. Warrior culture punishes code non-compliance at multiple levels.

As aggravating as this can be for many warriors, they have some comfort knowing that there exists an expected level of performance. But they also know that if they do not meet that level, the warrior culture has many ways to correct substandard performance or to bring painful consequences for violations.

This differs substantially from the civilian population, where failure to meet general standards often provokes little enforcement, and where even the transgression of genuine legal standards may bring little to no consequences. Veterans may feel significant culture shock when they return to a civilian environment and see many people living outside of a set code. They can feel even more aggravated when they see no way to enforce consequences for some lack of performance.

Similar episodes occur in both academic and civilian environments. I know of many former military service members who were sent to HR because they tried to enforce a consequence on someone who had failed to perform.

A We/Unit-Based Culture

As we have seen, the military intentionally tries to replace the individualistic mindset of recruits with a unit-based mindset. The goal is to stop them thinking only of themselves and instead to begin thinking of their effect on the group. Much of the military's initial conditioning is grounded in establishing this new mindset.

After a successful initial conditioning, the warrior culture continually reinforces this mindset. If a deployment or a training evolution takes place without one of the unit's warriors, guilt and shame are often used to gain compliance. Injured service members often leave the medical care they need so they can rejoin their unit in a combat zone (or even in training). This is no secret; it has been a common mindset throughout military history. It results from the we/unit-based mindset.

The individual warrior thinks not primarily of himself but of his friends and the unit he had to leave. Despite the potential worsening of a serious injury, he pushes to get back to his unit.

Early in the Iraq War, for example, I know of several snipers who had reached their End of Active Service (EAS) and were getting ready to leave the military. When they discovered a unit was getting ready to deploy to Iraq without any snipers in their battalion, three snipers about to leave the military instead extended their contracts to deploy with these units. This decision, of course, revealed a mix of the pride and honor-based culture as well as the unit-based culture.

The military ingrains in its warriors the obligation to think about the whole, not just the individual. I have heard thousands of stories of veterans sacrificing themselves to return to their units because of this unit-based mindset.

Here again, such a significant and entrenched mindset can create problems for the veteran transitioning back into a civilian culture. In general, civilians have a more self-focused mindset than those in the military. Civilian culture tends to be more individualistic: "Do what's best for you and your family." The culture shock occurs when a warrior re-enters a civilian environment and begins interacting with this individualistic mindset. While it most commonly happens in a workplace setting, it also takes place in both academic environments and social gatherings.

> Veterans commonly complain that their co-workers in the civilian environment think only of themselves, despite how it affects the team.

Veterans commonly complain that their co-workers in the civilian environment think only of themselves, despite how it affects the team. They must consciously work to fight the strong urge to correct such selfish/individualistic thinking. One former Cobra pilot who's been working in the corporate world for several years described it this way: "One of the most difficult things to get used to was people thinking only of themselves. They didn't really think of everybody in their unit or organization. They just thought about their own career and how it would benefit them. It can be really lonely when you're used to having people around you who are not concerned for your well-being."

I once worked with a combat veteran who had returned from Iraq. He had started college and was working at a popular fast-food chain. Due to his maturity and capability, management placed him at the head of the operations chain in the kitchen, a high stress position because of sheer demand. The stress and pressure of the job meant each person's role in this process was critical. If one person did not pull their weight, the whole team quickly noticed.

The veteran Marine recognized that one young college student did not pull his weight, which negatively affected everyone on the team. As a good Marine, he promptly corrected the problem. During his correction, he used aggressive language and may have told the employee that if he did not change his work ethic, he would have to "kill" him. Anyone from the warrior culture understands that such language merely expresses emphasis. This Marine, however, soon found himself sitting in front of the manager, advising him that he could not threaten people's lives. Fortunately, the incident did not lead to any greater consequence for this former warrior. It does, however, illustrate the culture shock brought on by returning to a civilian environment.

The freeway presents another frequent problem for warriors returning to civilian society. Incidents there can create unfortunate ramifications. A few common triggers can be traced to the unit-based mindset.

Many warriors frequently complain about other drivers, "They don't think of how their actions affect others." Many of these warriors seek to rectify such problematic situations and correct the individual driving in such an aggressive way. Such inconsiderate driving behavior also triggers the warrior's respect-based culture conditioning, especially when he or she feels disrespected because of someone's thoughtless freeway antics. The altercations that ensue can quickly escalate into situations that attract law enforcement.

The we/unit-based mindset is a significant factor in the worldview of a warrior. When that warrior re-enters the civilian world, the unit-based mindset often requires a very difficult adjustment.

An Aggression-Based Culture

At a Marine Corps boot camp graduation ceremony not long ago, I watched as young men marched in formation around the parade deck, proud and dignified as new warriors on their graduation day. As they circled the parade deck, appropriately filled with pride, a commentator described to the audience—mostly family members and friends (civilians)—what had been given to these young Marines.

"Your young Marines have been instilled with duty, honor, integrity," he said. The commentator walked through a whole catalog of values that, for the most part, our culture considers virtues. But then he interjected one term that most civilians would not consider a virtue: aggressiveness. Civilian culture tends to correlate aggressiveness with anger management, domestic violence, and other social problems.

Warrior culture, however, highly values aggressiveness.

Before basic training, many recruits have never been in a physical altercation with another human being. In basic training, however, these young warriors get thrust into various situations to learn to display aggressiveness toward other humans, even to the point of killing them. Soldiers training for war must be trained to do this, of course, but sometimes we forget the long-term ramifications of such training. While aggressiveness is a fundamental virtue for a warrior, what happens when the warrior re-enters the civilian world? There, aggressiveness can become a fundamental problem.

In my own boot camp, we had a practice called "combat hits." You stepped into a 4 by 4 boxing ring and had to wail on another human. You would get one minute of swinging and hitting the other guy, while the other guy tries to dodge and block. The roles are switched for another minute, and then drill instructors let the two warriors go free-for-all for a final minute. Three minutes may sound like a short time, but when you're swinging punches as hard as you can, trying to harm your opponent, it can be quite exhausting. I still remember my drill instructors telling us that if anybody made their opponent bleed, the one who drew blood was guaranteed a phone call home. Talk about making young men bloodthirsty!

I still remember my free-for-all. I caught a good right hook on my opponent's nose. I did not see the blood at first because I was too busy dodging and swinging. But once the contest ended, I saw blood flowing out of my opponent's nose. You would think I had scored the winning touchdown in a championship football game, the way I reacted.

Before entering the military, I did not consider myself an especially aggressive person. But the Marines instilled in me such powerful conditioning that I developed a thirst for aggression, along with the sense of feeling powerful that came with that aggression.

Is it any surprise, then, that intimate aggression rates among veterans are far above the national average? Veterans double the national average, and those rates quadruple for combat veterans. When you understand the aggressive nature of military culture and then apply that understanding to what takes place in the homes of these warriors, it is not hard to predict such a dramatic increase. The effect intensifies with a warrior's exposure to combat.

Warriors often bring the military's aggressive culture into their homes, even after they leave active duty. While we all know that a man cannot treat his wife and children like he treated fellow warriors, the conditioning is hard to break. It's like training a dog to be aggressive for fighting, and then expecting the same dog to become docile and amenable to children when in a different environment. Not all warriors struggle with this issue, of course; some effectively compartmentalize such aggressive behavior to the appropriate environments. But for many veterans the lines do get blurred.

Please do not imagine I'm condoning the aggressive behavior of warriors who, outside of military combat zones, harm loved ones or others. I raise this issue so we can better understand why some warriors behave with inappropriate aggression in the home. It is not due to some mental instability of the warrior, but often occurs because these warriors are acting exactly how they were trained to act. It's very hard to "turn off" such conditioning.

An Alcohol-Based Culture

The military in general is a strongly alcohol-based culture. While each warrior culture emphasizes alcohol to one degree or another, it's universal throughout the military. Why is it such a common cultural value?

The warrior culture is a high stress environment and warriors need to cope somehow with that stress. Throughout military history, alcohol has been known to provide an immediate release of stress. The basic nature of alcohol as a chemical depressant explains why it is used to relieve stress. Alcohol depresses the system and relaxes it.

Not every warrior who drinks regularly self-medicates for stress, of course. Many warriors engage in social drinking merely to have a good time. Still, we see a cultural norm in the military that takes place around alcohol. Many traditions also encourage the consumption of alcohol.

Regulations help to create this scenario. Federal military service members are not permitted to use any depressant drug for recreational purposes other than alcohol. While tobacco and caffeine are allowed, no other addictive drug or vice is permitted. Using other drugs can get a warrior kicked out of the military with an other-than-honorable discharge. Warriors therefore commonly use alcohol to cope with the stress. This not to say that they should be allowed to use other substances to deal with stress, but to illustrate how the military becomes an alcohol-based culture.

If a warrior suffers from some stress disorder, self-medicating with alcohol can intensify the problem. Taking psychotropic medication would typically run afoul of the pride-based culture. While today's military more readily accepts the use of physician-administered psychotropic medication, warriors tend to resist it because of their ingrained performance-based mentality.

Alcohol also plays a huge role in culturally bonding experiences. Many warriors regularly go out and suffer together and then afterwards go out drinking together. It's an expected part of the bonding process. If one warrior won't drink with another, it's often said that warrior cannot be trusted. I've heard warriors give countless anecdotal reasons why they need to be able to drink with fellow warriors to trust them.

Once a warrior leaves the military, personal alcohol use can create its own culture shock. How? The military culture that kept alcohol abuse and dependence in check is no longer present. Even in the military, some warriors go too far and must get substance-abuse treatment, but the very real threat of getting kicked out of the armed services or a reduction in rank because of substance abuse is enough to either keep it hidden or keep it in check. And let's face it, an 0530 morning run helps sober you up, as well. When warriors leave the military culture, they also leave all its boundaries, and some warriors cannot safely use the stress-reducing tool of alcohol without those boundaries.

We often see this problem among veterans as they make the transition into the civilian world. When their personal stress level increases significantly, they begin to use alcohol primarily for stress relief—when individuals use a pleasure-inducing substance to self-medicate over a long time, it is always a recipe for disaster.

One tragic consequence of this culture shock is a high rate of suicide. Substance abuse, combined with owning firearms, is a primary indicator of the potential for suicide. When warriors struggle with their transition to civilian culture and choose to regularly use alcohol to self-medicate, they depress their system from normal inhibitions. They therefore find it much easier to cross the threshold of action into suicide, especially when they have firearms readily available to make the action both quick and easy. Too many of our fellow warriors fall prey to the slippery slope of this stress-relieving coping mechanism..

It's Not What You May Think

Warrior culture is *not* merely a subculture of the larger civilian culture. While warrior culture operates within the American civilian culture, it exhibits all the characteristics of a primary culture.

This means that warriors who leave the military culture should recognize that they may not be able to walk back into the civilian culture as readily as they might imagine. It simply is not that easy, on many levels. Warriors should expect to suffer significant culture shock in multiple arenas of life. Assimilating back into the civilian culture will require them to change themselves at their very core. For many, these changes are too difficult to manage on their own.

As a warrior myself, I have experienced the difficult transition from active duty to veteran. For most of my adult life, I also have worked with warriors on a clinical level. Both my personal experience and my ongoing work with veterans and active-duty service members has put a spotlight on the many problematic areas that tend to create a continuous flow of issues for veterans and service members. While I have not provided a comprehensive list of these challenges, I hope I have described enough of them to demonstrate how *years* of warrior conditioning can make it difficult to successfully transition to civilian life.

Three Big Challenges

In the next three chapters, I want to highlight and describe three of the biggest challenges warriors face when they try to re-enter the civilian world. Some of us struggle more with these issues than others, but we all must prepare ourselves for the significant challenges to come. To be forewarned is to be fore-armed.

I have found the following three areas to be critical to any successful transition. Navigating these three areas well will enable the warrior to effectively adapt back into the civilian culture. Since these three areas appear to create the most common and most difficult problems for individual warriors, I want to address each of them more extensively.

Pass and Review

- A performance-based culture needs a standard to perform to. When warriors leave the military, they lose the standard.
- Those who come from a respect culture find it easy to feel disrespected in the civilian culture.
- A warrior's pride often becomes a barrier to reaching out and getting help when needed.
- The warrior culture is a "we" driven culture and directly conflicts with the "individual" civilian culture.
- While aggression is intentionally instilled to equip the warrior for war, that aggression is not reconditioned to be more appropriate for other areas of life.
- Military culture uses alcohol to celebrate and to deal with stress and creates its own boundaries with alcohol use. When the boundaries are lifted, however, the barriers to self-destruction are removed.

Inspection

1. How do you know if you are performing successfully in the civilian world?

2. What types of behaviors make you feel disrespected in the civilian world?

3. How do you view "getting help?" Do you see it as a form of weakness? Explain.

4. How do you feel when someone thinks only of themselves in their actions?

5. How easily do you act aggressively when pushed?

6. Which areas of culture shock are you most prone to, or will be prone to?

11

Performance and Shame

When we don't have a clear standard of what we
to perform to, the unfortunate result is shaming
ourselves for not meeting the unclear standard.

I've already mentioned three key tools often used in the military to get individuals to conform to cultural standards: pain, shame, and paperwork. Of the three, the most insidious and effective is shame.

The performance-based warrior culture brings to bear both public and personal shaming whenever a member fails to perform acceptably. Every performance-based, honor-based culture uses shaming to gain compliance; the military is no exception. Shame and avoidance of shame are powerful motivators, especially in a communal culture such as the military. And in the military, the power of shame intensifies.

> *Every* performance-based, honor-based culture uses shaming to gain compliance; the military is no exception.

A Shameful Experience

In the second phase of boot camp, we felt more like Marines than we did in the first phase. It had started to become our identity, which we loved.

In the Marines, someone always remains on watch over the barracks. One day, another recruit and I were on watch at the barracks while the rest of our platoon was out practicing drill. A few sergeants came by, identified themselves as base maintenance personnel, and told us we needed to make some corrections and then notify our drill instructors about them. The sergeants met us outside and pointed out several discrepancies.

Once we returned to our appointed place of duty inside, we discovered that someone had entered the barracks in our absence and basically destroyed it. Oddly, the only thing the person had stolen was a single sheet (the fart sack). When our drill instructors returned, we informed them what had happened—and for the remainder of the day, they proceeded to thrash us. We had to repeat, screaming at the top of our lungs, the general order, "I will not leave my post unless properly relieved."

After several hours of such physical correction (pain), we felt exhausted. The drill instructors then gathered around us the rest of our platoon and loudly emphasized our failure. They used this public shaming time to teach the rest of the platoon what *not* to do.

As I look back on this event, I see it clearly as a staged event, no doubt involving our drill instructors. It powerfully influenced our unit because *no one* wanted to endure that type of intense shaming. While the physical pain of the event dissipated shortly afterward, my feelings of shame and embarrassment still resonate deeply, even to this day. I remember glancing up at my peer group and seeing them look at me with disdain because of my lack of performance and honor.

After these shaming events, our drill instructors had a recovery process for recruits who had failed. A drill instructor pulled me aside after a few days of agony and depression and walked me through how to rebuild myself and to avoid such shame in the future. While it was a powerful experience for me, it was not an isolated one. Events like these are common practice.

Such conditioning results in a very shame-aversive culture. Individual Marines will do whatever it takes to avoid non-performance that might bring them communal shame. While not every warrior has the same degree of shame aversion, warriors typically try hard to avoid the deepest levels of shame. One former force recon Marine pointed this out:

> "I think that the shame response is a massively important tool when it comes to the military. And I think of a current movement in the

military that says, 'You can't shame people.' But I am telling you, if people lose their shame response, that's it. The culture loses its control when it tries to instill proper conduct and behavior."

Whether we like it or not, shame has a role to play in the formation of warriors.

Research Among Males

Shame aversion is not an issue merely among warriors. It is very common for men in general to feel very sensitive to shame. This makes sense because the warrior culture does not make things up out of nowhere. Rather, it takes what it finds among civilians and transforms it into something that better suits the warrior function. Not only would it be much more difficult to create something out of nothing but intensifying a drive already present is *far* more potent and effective.

Multiple studies have shown that men are far more responsive to shame than women. Nevertheless, women trained in warrior culture also are conditioned to respond to shame, even though men tend to respond to it much more naturally. Males naturally connect shame to whatever standard/performance/significance they consider their highest value. Whenever they fail to perform in these value areas, they feel shame. This response to shame is also powerful in how the community accepts or rejects behaviors or individuals.

These value areas vary significantly among men; they might attach their standard of performance or significance to almost anything. The warrior culture transforms this general sense of shame and places all of it in just one standard, the one selected by the military. This new standard is then exalted far beyond anything else, and when a warrior does not perform according to the standard, that warrior naturally feels a powerful sense of deep shame. This makes more sense when you understand the deep, ingrained warrior ethos and code as described earlier.

Young recruits in boot camp nearing final completion of their crucible must go without sleep and food as they tackle difficult tasks. This creates a cauldron ripe for instilling a value system. Throughout the several days of the crucible, in which all these difficult tasks take place, there come intermittent periods of describing battlefield citations for the medal of honor. Most warriors receive this medal posthumously.

All these recruits hear repeatedly about selfless sacrifice for the benefit of the unit, and/or recordings of tremendous acts of courage and valor. As these sleep-deprived and hungry young warriors hear these stirring histories, even as they accomplish some of the most difficult things they've ever tried to do, military standards of performance and honor are deeply instilled in them. A powerful value system takes root. They now have a clear standard of how they should perform in unimaginable situations. They have a standard for how they must strive to operate and perform when they find themselves in similar situations.

Shame Response and Suicide

Much research shows shame is a very common cause of depression in men that often causes feelings of helplessness, inadequacy, failure, and self-deficiency. One researcher claimed that it is hard to distinguish shame from depression.[x] Other research states that "maladaptive coping strategies like self-punishment and cognitive social avoidance are positively related to suicide ideation."[xi] A growing body of research shows that a shame response co-existing with depression is directly correlated with suicidal ideation experienced by many veterans and active-duty warriors..

Thomas Joiner has researched suicide for many years. He has identified the conditions under which a person is most likely to attempt suicide. The idea that shame connected with depression often leads to suicide ideation corresponds closely to Joiner's theory of suicide ideation. His theory speaks of two primary drivers of suicidal motivation. The first is feelings of burdensomeness (intra-personal) and the second is feelings of low belongingness (inter-personal). A third component causes the thought of suicide to reach critical phases: the "acquired capacity for suicide" (also called "heightened capability to inflict harm" on oneself). When the first two drivers combine with the third component, a lethal situation often results.

Without question, the military shame response correlates with feelings of burdensomeness. Many veterans also feel isolated once they disconnect from their units, so they experience low belongingness. When these two factors combine with the ability to inflict violence (conditioned from boot camp), no fear of firearms, and a greater capacity for violence, a perfect

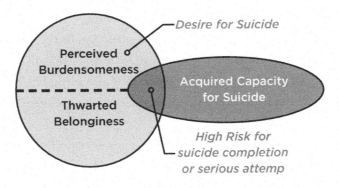

Thomas Johner's model of suicide risk, 2006

recipe exists for veterans to make fatal decisions.

James Bond Stockdale, an independent candidate for Vice President of the United States in 1992, was a highly decorated veteran. He received two Distinguished Flying Crosses, three Distinguished Service Medals, two Purple Hearts, and the Congressional Medal of Honor. He also served as president of the Naval War College, was a senior fellow of the Hoover Institute, and held eight honorary degrees. He wrote, "Shame is heavy, a heavier burden than any physical wounds ... the thing that brings down a man is not pain but shame"[xii] This decorated warrior highlights the power of shame and in his books writes more about it.

A veteran I've worked with also has a lot to say about shame. He connects the feeling of shame with perfectionism and describes how it worked in his own experience:

"Oh yeah, 100 percent, shame and failure. I think because we were made to be perfectionists, not all are, but 90 percent are. We're such perfectionists that 95 percent effort can feel like failure to us. That's the way we were made to be, and that can be very detrimental. I've seen suicides because of it. They are performing great, but they don't feel like they're doing it.

"I had a guy, while I was on the drill field, who wasn't gonna qualify on the range. Phenomenal Marine and great leader, a little bit older. Everything's rocking and rolling for him, but he's not going to qualify on the range. So, I talked to him. I explained, "It's no big deal. You're gonna just recycle, go through the range again. You'll probably get it that time. Sometimes it takes dudes a little bit.

"Instead, on Pre Qual he stands up and pulls the trigger. And I know it was because he was going to fail at qualifying on the rifle. He was too ashamed to be pulled from that platoon and be dropped to another platoon as the guide. The shame was too powerful."

I cannot underemphasize the point: shame powerfully influences both active-duty warriors and veterans. For many, suicide becomes a way of "taking care of the problem" created by shame. When warriors view themselves as the problem, they often seek to address it through self-harm. Before this happens, we must work to turn down the response.

A Case Study in Shame
A History Channel show called The Selection showed fifty civilians who for eight days willingly subjected themselves to the torture of the selection process used by military special operations units. Multiple former special operations/Navy SEALs/force reconnaissance operators ran the training for the show. This reality program closely replicated many of the testing and proving protocols the military uses for those who want to join special operations.

The program demonstrated the many techniques typically used to weed out weak-minded and weak-bodied participants. One episode powerfully revealed how the military uses the power of shame to influence warriors. Keep in mind that these participants were not military personnel and had *not* joined the military, although some contestants who aspired to work in special operations wanted to use the show as a test.

In one of the final episodes called "Humility," one of the best performers of five remaining participants finally breaks. This participant, an exceptional physical specimen, throughout the competition had never been broken. In personal inventories he seemed to thrive off of physical pain. He always finished at the top of the performance/finish level and became the class leader.

As the class experiment went on, however, he fell prey to a classic tool of the warrior culture: to make an example of someone regarding the lesson of integrity. I strongly encourage you to watch this episode because it graphically reveals the staggering power of shame.

In brief, the participants were asked to perform several calisthenic tasks throughout a running course. No one physically monitored them and they were to report honestly how they did. In fact, it was a test of integrity.

Contestants did not know that instructors had placed cameras at each station to verify they had completed their assigned repetitions. They had anticipated that at least one participant would not complete the activities prescribed. After participants returned from the course for a time of rest, instructors called them in and notified them that one participant did not complete all assigned tasks. It turned out that the class leader, the physical stud, did not complete one of his assigned tasks. He then gets lectured on integrity and is threatened with physical punishment for his failure. At that point, the class leader breaks psychologically and is ready to quit, despite the support he receives from his fellow participants.

Here was an individual who could not be broken physically but who was susceptible to the psychological use of shame. I see this as a classic example of the power of shame as used in the warrior culture. Shame is an extraordinarily powerful tool used to get individuals to conform to the standards set for them. This civilian did not anticipate such psychological torment and ultimately got ambushed by it.

The story does not end there. Because the instructors came from the military, they used the class leader's failure as a tool to teach important lessons to the whole group—a common use of shame in the military.

The warrior culture almost never leaves a guilty warrior in a state of shame. It normally takes corrective measures that allow the warrior to redeem his or her honor. It gives warriors the structure they need to earn back their honor, and, more importantly, it uses the incident to advance the unity of the team.

When the show's instructors send the embarrassed individual to pay the price for his mistake, remaining team members joined him so that he did not have to bear the shame alone. This incident is tremendously powerful and illustrates the power of using shame for a constructive purpose.

Please do not view shame only as a destructive tool! In an honor-based culture, shame has a key function to uphold the society. Warrior cultures usually have some structures in place to correct errant behavior, which make the individual warrior and team even stronger.

Most problems with shame set in once warriors leave the military culture. Warriors who exit the culture that instilled this honor/shame-based response become very confused when they re-enter the civilian world. Standards of conduct often are not clear in civilian culture, outside of the legal rules instituted to keep general order. The standards of civilian life are often ambiguous and do not clearly lay out how one may perform optimally.

I often hear veterans lament how they feel like failures because they doubt their performance as fathers or husbands. Unclear standards in these areas cause them to feel shame for falling short, but they have no corrective measures to help them improve, as in the military. So, these men sit in shame, which only grows more powerful the longer they continue to remain in this state. Sometimes the ex-warrior begins to look at himself as the problem . . . and he may see only one way to resolve the problem. Because of a lack of structure and community that keeps the constructive nature of shame in check, dire consequences too often result.

What to Do?

Internalized shame is one of the most long-term, destructive forces the warrior culture can leave with veterans. It *must* be corrected or adjusted. Unrelieved self-shame can lead to isolation and depression, which never lead anywhere good.

> Internalized shame is one of the most long-term, destructive forces the warrior culture can leave with veterans. It must be corrected or adjusted.

So, what can a veteran do with a shame response deeply instilled from the warrior culture? Allow me to suggest some insights that veterans can begin to gain from immediately.

Although the warrior culture uses shame as a powerful tool to get its warriors to perform well under extreme scenarios, it also uses collective and productive measures to bring about beneficial results. We can see this illustrated in The Selection program described earlier. Instructors on the show used the shame of one participant to create a team-building tool.

After using the contestant's shame to highlight the importance of integrity and to correct and teach the embarrassed man a key lesson, they gave him specific details on how to correct his behavioral deficiency by performing a task. Through the successful completion of this task, the individual could redeem himself and return to performance and honor.

In this case, they required him to complete a full course of the fifty burpees that he had failed to complete earlier. Then they used the man's tough time to enhance the team's bond. All remaining participants voluntarily completed the exercise with the shamed team leader in what amounted to a corporate/communal way to release his shame.

It does not always work out this way in the warrior culture, of course. At times the shame tool can be greatly abused. Most often, however, in the end it has a tremendously positive impact on the individual and a greatly beneficial impact on the team.

Dealing with Shame in the Civilian World

How are veterans to effectively deal with the shame response once they return to the civilian world? I have attended many conferences focused on clinical skills for dealing with shame, as well as reading several books on this topic, but all are written for the civilian culture. None of them take into account how much the warrior identity is tied to the honor and shame response. Many warriors therefore will not accept the advice given through such channels, because their counsel appears to challenge or even insult the warrior identity.

Most current clinical interventions for shame concern self-compassion or mindfulness to better regulate emotions. While this may work for some, many of these treatments seek to devalue or dismiss shame. This is very difficult for the warrior to do, however, because shame is tied to the warrior identity.

I believe veterans must instead begin to adapt to our current circumstance what we learned in the military. We need to find our answers in the powerful identity that warriors receive in the military and then adapt them for our use in this new phase of life.

1. Understand why the shame response exists and how it works within us.
Such an understanding helps us to separate ourselves from the instilled shame response. We do not try to degrade the purpose of shame in the warrior culture, but rather we try to understand it and adapt it to our new scenario in life.

2. Become aware of when you tend to react with a shame response.
Only with time and intentional awareness can you begin to catch yourself whenever you start reacting with shame. Think of it as an ambush. The first time you get caught in an ambush, it surprised you and you felt as though it came out of nowhere. The more experience you got and the more ambushes you survived, however, you started to slow down the process and began to recognize all the subtle triggers that led up to it. You began to notice all the details, like fewer people in the marketplace, the common responses of locals, terrain features often used in ambushes. Over time, you could recognize the ambush before it happened—but it took time, experience, and intentional awareness to reach that point.

I often sit with veterans to help them identify the triggers that tend to take place before they blow up in a shame response. For instance, before the response reaches the anger explosion, we work to help them see that they usually react to the shame through defensiveness. This is often a feeling like guilt, or that they have done something wrong.

Second, we identify the thoughts driving the response. This is important because it is the catalyst that ignites the anger. Certain precursors make the reaction more likely, such as high stress circumstances. Warriors under high stress often hold themselves to a high standard of performance, which makes them more prone to become irritable and to react by mistreating loved ones. When we are under high stress, we also have less emotional energy to react tactfully. When precursors like high stress start showing up, we must identify our thoughts that drive poor responses, or we will act in ways that create more shame.

One final note: the most common reaction to shame is not cowering or a melancholy feeling, but rather an explosion of anger. The warrior culture has conditioned us to deal with our negative emotions primarily through anger. Shame is nearly the same; when the warrior feels shame, it often comes out in an explosive, angry response.

3. How do you react after your shame response?

After warriors respond with shame to some incident, their most common reaction is to isolate themselves. They begin to push away from those toward whom they feel the most shame. The family man who yells at his wife or blows up at his kids over something small usually isolates himself and then stews in his shame. Outsiders, and especially his wife and kids, believe the warrior is angry with them, when in fact he feels extremely aggravated and disappointed with himself. Many times, he has no awareness of what is taking place until he notices that he has begun to shame himself.

The warrior who feels such shame cannot allow himself to sit in it for long. Yes, he may need time to calm himself and regulate his emotions, but once he has calmed down on a physiological level, he needs to go back and address the issue. Regardless of whether the incident took place with family, coworkers, a boss, parents, or within any other relational dynamic, he must get up and reconnect with them.

At times the incident occurs in a non-relational setting and the veteran cannot reconnect with the parties involved. If the veteran blew up on the freeway and tried to run somebody off the road or challenge someone to a fight, we want to help him snap out of the isolating behavior. Isolation and stewing on negative emotion become the petri dish for shame to grow and multiply. If the veteran remains in this isolation for long periods, over the years, it affects the warrior's entire psyche. He will begin to look at himself as if he is a burden to others and the cause of the problem.

The action step here is to make sure the veteran does not sit and stew in the shame. If you have become more aware of what is happening and you calm down to see it more clearly, then you must force yourself out of the isolation. Do not go to alcohol to numb the pain, which only makes the response more powerful once the alcohol wears off. Instead, move to the next step of this process.

4. For an inter-relational issue, the warrior must apologize for his/her outburst.

Warriors often find this step one to be the most difficult. In the warrior culture, apologies are seldom given verbally, but usually through actions. In the civilian world, however, the relationship itself must be repaired, not merely the fixing of some inappropriate action. This requires adaptation.

More importantly, the loved ones targeted by the veteran's outburst must understand that *they* did not cause the rage. I often teach veterans that this step parallels taking ownership of their actions. In the warrior culture, taking ownership for one's actions is part of the warriors' code. It is expected that warriors will take ownership/responsibility for the mistakes once they have received the appropriate consequences.

In the civilian world, they must do a similar thing in their relational interactions. They must take ownership for their outburst, which they do by giving an apology. So, take responsibility of your actions and apologize for the way you reacted.

A common belief in the warrior culture holds that apologies signify weakness. Warriors are taught instead to correct their behavior. I can't count how often I have heard this line of argument in couples' therapy. The spouse wants a veteran to recognize and apologize for what he's done, but the veteran believes he already has apologized because he has corrected his behavior and done something to make up for it. I always tell the warrior, "Take ownership and apologize. That is the new standard." When the apology gets consciously connected to the code of leadership, it makes more sense to the veteran.

5. Correct the problem.

The warrior culture usually provides an opportunity to correct problems through appropriate actions. If the warrior is criminally charged, of course, the infraction takes on a whole different scale. Here we have in mind the re-training and re-conditioning of the warrior in the absence of some legal issue.

The UCMJ provides for the correction of minor infractions of military culture. It may restrict personnel to quarters. The warrior may have to check in with the duty officer every four hours, twenty-four hours a day, and always in uniform. They are never allowed the luxury of getting out of uniform, and even in the middle of the night they must check in. During such a restriction, they cannot go anywhere except chow and PT. I have known many warriors who have received this form of correction and then been allowed to earn back their rank.

This task gets more complicated after returning to a civilian environment. How do you identify what you must do to correct unacceptable behavior? In the military, your command/direct superiors identify for you what must do to correct the behavior and make up for it. But who in an ambiguous civilian situation can identify those specifics? Nevertheless, the warrior must be made to feel that he has corrected the problem.

I've seen many individuals ignore this issue, only to become more sensitive to the shame as the years go by. The anger responses sparked by the problem only increase over time. Conversely, if they can address the issue and correct the behavior through some type of action, a release of shame usually follows.

I once worked with a highly decorated combat veteran who late one night drove under the influence of alcohol. He ran into several parked cars but kept on driving, fearful of the consequence of a DUI. The veteran never told anyone about the incident, and it took several months before he spoke about it to me. He had freely described many combat traumas but carefully hid this deepest area of his shame. It felt more deeply personal to him than anything else and seemed very difficult to reveal.

Once he finally confessed his infraction, we walked through the process of repairing the damage. When we reached the step of identifying what he could do to make up for his behavior, he reported that he had returned to the area to look for the damaged cars, but he could not find them. No doubt, they had been replaced. We had to get creative to figure out how he could release the shame.

We decided that he could return to the neighborhood and offer his services to the local residents (he owned a handyman company). We specified a certain amount of money that he would essentially "donate" through his labor to the community. Once he reached that level, he felt a sense of release, feeling that he had made right his wrong.

Every case will be different, of course, but every warrior must come to understand that they need to make some appropriate correction for the wrongs they commit. They also must come to know the power of release made possible by their correction. They must find appropriate ways within the civilian culture to repair the shame they feel.

Stop Sitting in Shame

I am convinced that the failure to deal with shame is one of the dominant reasons for the high suicide level among our veteran population. It's not because of PTSD, though this no doubt contributes to the problem. We condition our warriors to value honor and to loathe shame, and far too many of our veterans continue to sit alone, immersed in shame.

Eventually they conclude that they are the problem and so take violent action to correct the problem.

This must change!

As Smedley Butler wrote, "Too many of these fine young boys are destroyed mentally, because they could not make the final about-face alone."

We must help them to make that final about-face. Shame does not have to destroy them! They have been soaking in shame, all by themselves, for far too long.

Pass and Review

- Shame is a potent tool to get young recruits to conform to military norms.
- Desire for the acceptance of one's community intensifies the power of shame.
- Shame is often the single greatest factor that causes of the decision to follow through with a suicide attempt.
- Shame outside of the warrior culture becomes like a fire leaping out of a fire pit; it can grow out of control.
- Steps to relieve shame:
- Be aware of it
- Catch yourself doing it
- Don't sit in it
- Apologize for it
- Fix it.

Inspection

1. Describe a time you were shamed for a lack of performance or honor. Have you ever shamed anyone for their lack of performance? Explain.

2. Describe a time when you felt the lack of acceptance from your community.

3. Have you ever got to the place where you thought it would be better for others if you were not here? Explain.

4. What actions could you take to find relief from the shame response?

12

★ ★ ★

Loss of Significance

To live for a mission that is bigger than yourself is fulfilling.
To lose this purpose and be acutely aware
of what you are missing is devastating.

Loss of purpose is the second critical area that causes great psychological disruption for warriors after they leave the military. To understand why this is so, you must understand several key things about the warrior mentality.

Living with Purpose

Warriors live with a commitment to purpose, to something greater than themselves and outside of themselves. The warrior culture is meant to serve a very specific purpose, a calling that can create tremendous difficulty for warriors after they leave the service.

So, what's the problem? Many veterans have trouble identifying a purpose in their new life that comes anywhere close to approaching the great purpose they had in their old life. And that lack of a new, worthwhile purpose causes problems for them.

Imagine that you lived your entire life in a tiny community of 250 residents who eked out their living on the edge of a blistering desert. No one ever visits your town, and no resident ever leaves it. One day, though, you look up at some birds flying far overhead and you start wondering where they came from. You keep pondering the lives of those birds, and within a few weeks, you decide to track them down. Despite severe warnings from the village elders, you pack up a few things and leave town. In a few days, you walk and hitchhike your way to a faraway valley, lush and green and teeming with friendly people. They take a liking to you, give you a job, train you how to do it, and instruct you on how life works in their valley, which they call Mission Critical. You spend several years there and one day wake up with a desire to visit your hometown. You're not the same person now that you were back when you left, but you fondly recall the close-knit community, the clear skies, and the stars shining brightly in the desert sky. By then, you own a car, and you drive "home" . . . and the moment you arrive, you feel desperately out of place. The people there talk differently than you do now, walk different, think different, live different.

Do you suppose it would be easy for you to move back there, for good?

The townspeople appear to like having you there again, but you can hear them whispering behind your back: "What's gotten into *him*? I believe he thinks he's better than us! And do you see the way he looks at our town? He's changed, but not for the better."

Without stretching the metaphor too far, I hope you see the point. When warriors live in the warrior culture and are being used to accomplish a greater purpose, to serve their country, they usually enjoy a deep sense of fulfillment. Many Warriors have no idea how deep that sense of fulfillment has grown until after they get out and they don't have it anymore. When a warrior returns to the civilian world without this sense of fulfillment, a crushing sense of disillusionment often sets in, along with a numbing effect. You feel a little nostalgic the first few days you're back "home" in the desert, but soon you can't help but wonder, *Is this all there is?* Many warriors believe they will never again feel the sense of significance they had in the military, of being part of something much bigger than themselves.

I've known many warriors who have made energetic attempts to regain that sense of significance by making a lot of money or chasing other self-focused dreams, only to end up disappointed and frustrated. The civilian world does not lack significant missions or purpose, but those who want such significance have to work hard to identify what avenue of purpose they should pursue, and how they can know without a doubt that it is significant.

In the military, you don't have to wonder and you don't have to choose. You are provided with both your mission and the resources required to accomplish it. Not so in the civilian world.

Man's Search for Meaning

All humans seek for meaning and purpose. It's fundamental to human existence. We've already mentioned Victor Frankel, whose time in a Nazi concentration camp during World War II set him on a lifelong career to discover the staggering role that purpose and meaning play in all human life.

When we sense no meaning or purpose in our lives, we feel an interior, existential vacuum, a hollowness, an emptiness, or a void that shrivels the soul. That emptiness can lead to hopelessness that causes some individuals to lose the will to live.

A well-regarded research article concludes that combat experience can intensify a warrior's need for meaning and purpose: "War experiences hit the core of the existential experience, but even in great sorrow and suffering there is meaning, underscoring that meaning is crucial to sustaining life. Humans always have the choice to find it. Accordingly, a resilient approach replaces the combat experience within a meaningful life context."[xiii] Combat experience can have a tremendous impact on meaning and purpose, even if that purpose was only to keep your friends alive.

Many warriors experience great difficulty when they lose the single arena in which they found great meaning and purpose. The military assigns them this purpose, and the combat situations they experience force them to fight for that purpose.

When they return to the civilian world . . . what then? Will it fulfill them to live a relatively comfortable life, yet without much meaning or purpose?

An article from *The Journal of The American Association of Suicidology* published a study that shocked many mental health workers. The article, titled "Does reintegration stress contribute to suicide ideation among returning veterans seeking PTSD treatment," highlights the loss of meaning and purpose as a fundamental component of increased suicidal ideation. The authors state, "Logistic regressions indicate that reintegration stress has a unique effect on suicide ideation over and above PTSD and depression symptoms. The authors of this article found that this reintegration stress created more suicidal ideation than PTSD or depression symptoms combined. The questions are, "What is the reintegration stress' and 'what are its components?"[xiv]

The authors defined reintegration of stress as "types of reintegration difficulties associated with suicide ideation," including "difficulty maintaining military friendships, difficulty getting along with relatives, difficulty feeling like you belong in civilian society, and difficulty finding meaning and purpose in life." All of these were "significantly associated with suicidal ideation."

Do you see why it makes sense that such "reintegration stress" tends to present such difficulties for the veteran? In my clinical work, I have found that when veterans lack a useful and meaningful sense of purpose, they begin to flounder in life. With this floundering comes frustration and anger, which often flares against loved ones. When warriors have no mission, they have nothing that pushes them to stay sharp.

Anybody who's served in the military knows that when you leave young warriors alone with nothing to do, it's only a matter of time before they get into trouble. Many of the military's key leadership principles detail how to keep service members appropriately engaged. In the military it seems especially true that "idle hands are the devil's playground."

Let me suggest an experiment. Go to YouTube and look up "bored military service members." In seconds you will witness some of the most creative and destructive things that warriors do when they lack an actionable purpose.

Resilience and Purpose

Now let's move from a focus on pathology to a focus on performance. Steven Southwick, in both his book and research, identifies several key components of resilience. One of the primary components of resilience, he says, is a sense of meaning and purpose.

"In psychological research," he writes, "studies have found that having a clear and valued purpose, and committing fully to a mission, can markedly strengthen one's resilience." Service members gain a greater sense of resilience when they have a deeper sense of meaning and purpose.

I commonly hear from veterans that when they were still on active duty, they did not feel the impact of these problems of purpose and did not seem to be as affected by them as after they left the military. They had lost many key factors of resilience, loss of purpose among the biggest of them. Losing that sense of purpose makes them less capable to bounce back after difficulty or persevere through hardship.

Southwick also identifies "living a meaningful life" as "a basic human need, without which we can easily fall into despair, alienation, or even violent acts against others or ourselves." Unfortunately, this is exactly what we see happening when some active-duty warriors re-enter the civilian culture. Southwick believes so deeply in the strength of this factor that he has made extensive efforts in working with veterans through the VA to use a type of therapy that helps these veterans regain a sense of meaning and purpose. The problem with this approach is that it typically focuses on only those clinically diagnosed with PTSD, which means that, once again, we bump up against the idea that only some pathology creates the need for treatment.

The message must grow much larger. *All* warriors transitioning to life in the civilian world must find meaning and purpose in that world if they are to succeed, grow, and thrive.

> *All* warriors transitioning to life in the civilian world must find meaning and purpose in that world if they are to succeed, grow, and thrive

Marriage Education and the Male Drive

In my master's work on marriage, I gained tremendous insights about men and women and their commonalities and differences. One issue very relevant to the military experience is the primary internal need that both men and women have to feel significance in life. While they both have this need, they express it quite differently.

In the case of the military, an external authority tells a man what his upmost value is. This differs from many females, whose primary internal drive is for security. While this can vary among individuals, in general, this pattern remains quite stable. I've sat in thousands of sessions with couples, hearing them describe their situations, and in the vast majority of cases this pattern keeps reappearing. Please understand this drive is not meant to be a drive for selfishness or arrogance, but a drive to feel that what they are doing really matters.

In general, men serving in the military as part of the warrior culture automatically get a sense of satisfaction that they are using their life in a significant way. While some feel disgruntled because of their job or profession, most of those who join the military do so because they want to feel a sense of significance.

I often see a similar scenario play out with females who are conditioned in the same way (and often have the same complaints). We are wired to feel a sense of significance. When we have had it and then we lose it, we find it a very difficult situation to tolerate.

A Great Loss Not Immediately Recognized

When military personnel leave the armed services and thus lose the significant purpose that comes with being a warrior, often they don't immediately recognize how much they have lost. Individuals who gain a sense of significance from their military service by being involved in something much bigger than themselves tend not to anticipate the shock when they no longer have the active stimulation of such service.

While civilian culture may value the military's purpose, it doesn't carry nearly the same weight as being active in it yourself. I've noticed this phenomenon repeatedly after working with thousands of veterans. One of the major difficulties for someone leaving the military is the loss of a greater sense of purpose. We miss the sense that we are part of something bigger than ourselves.

Having a family and providing for that family provides a tremendous purpose, but it seldom feels to the veteran as significant as protecting a nation. It becomes a role naturally assumed, like most civilians, and at some level it often feels less fulfilling than serving in the military. That's not to say that this evaluation is always accurate; it is, however, the experience of many service members.

When I work with veterans, after we address injuries and begin to re-orient expectations for civilian life, we talk about purpose and significance. We discuss where the veteran will find significance outside of the military. Veterans need to understand that significance and purpose will no longer be assigned to them; they must now assign these things to themselves, which means they must identify what they consider worth living for.

When we find something worth living for, make a commitment to it, and are willing to sacrifice for it, we naturally assign value to it. Once we've assigned a value to this purpose, it will begin to bring us a sense of significance.

It is often a very difficult process to help warriors find their own sense of purpose, primarily because they are used to having their sense of purpose dictated to them. Many veterans almost come to believe that they cannot assign to themselves their own sense of purpose, that it must come from some external entity. With time and exploration, however, they come to see that they control what would serve as a meaningful purpose for them; but this process takes hard work. You must be aware of your need for something if you are going to work hard for it.

The Need to Get Involved

I often begin my work with veterans by trying to get them involved with *something*. Together, we try to identify a need that they see in the world. We start with needs because needs usually drive purpose. Then we look at needs they see in the world that personally motivate them.

Once we identify such a need, we begin to look at the veteran's specific skill set that could meet this need. We look for like-minded people or agencies that already do this type of significant work. We begin to align veterans with social support and other individuals who may have the same passion as they do.

When we begin to live out a purpose, we come alive again. If warriors continue to accept a life without purpose, they will flounder and grow discouraged. Moving from a life of significance and purpose to a life where one's significance and purpose lie only in the past will *always* lead to depression or despair.

Find a New Summit

Veterans must accept that while their military service was a summit, they will never again be on that same summit. They can, however, reach a different summit.

Every warrior must take the critical step of acceptance. Many warriors believe that serving in the military was one of the most significant things they've ever done. All generations of warrior cultures share this belief.

I have the great privilege of working with warriors from all generations of our nation's battle legacy. I typically ask Vietnam and World War II veterans to think of the three most significant things they've ever done. Not one veteran has ever omitted "the war" as one of the most significant experiences of his life. But significant does not mean it was pleasant or easy! Even fifty to seventy years after their wartime experience, these veterans still get together in groups to talk about what they went through, incorporating both good and bad memories.

> Veterans must accept that while their military service was a summit, they will never again be on that same summit. They can, however, reach a different summit.

When I work with younger warriors, we must get to the point where they accept that their military experience has ended and a transition must take place. I often use the metaphor of a mountain summit to describe their military service. For the warrior, serving in the military was a high point, a mountain top summit. But the time comes when they must come down off that summit and find a new path for the rest of their life. They will never return to that summit, but that does not mean they must live out their days in the valleys. When they find a new purpose to live for, they can reach a new summit, equally as high and sometimes even more breathtaking.

They will never reach that next summit, however, if they continue to sit in the valley, wishing they were back on the last summit. Part of getting to the new summit is identifying a new purpose for which they can live.

I've seen it hundreds of times with veterans who learn to adapt to their new environment. When they find a purpose they are willing to live for, they adapt the warrior spirit to fit the new endeavor. This new purpose brings a great sense of satisfaction and meaning to their lives.

Unfortunately, many young warriors, and sometimes old warriors, never make this adaptation. They try to live in past glories. It doesn't work well, and it's no way to live.

Finding a new purpose is not easy. The hardest part is identifying what makes a veteran passionate and connecting that passion to some new purpose. Veterans do this in various ways. Most warriors find this passion either through giving back to other warriors or through faith-based practices. In these two very natural ways many warriors begin to identify their new purpose. They have taken these proven paths to find significance once more.

Pass and Review

- Once you have lived with purpose you are far more aware of what you are missing when you no longer have it.
- We are built for purpose; without it we will flounder in life.
- The loss of a clear purpose is one of the ways that warriors struggle when they get out of the military.
- Having meaning and purpose to your life is what gives you the resilience to bounce back after difficulties. It is much harder to remain resilient when you have no purpose driving you.
- All of us have a deep internal drive to feel significant.
- You will not be aware of what you lost until you no longer have it; and then you will struggle to know how to get it back.
- Contemplate that your past purpose is over and identify some new purpose that you will live for.

Inspection

1. What are you living for now that you are out of the military?
2. Was purpose did you find in the military that felt significant to you?
3. What meaningful purpose have you found since you left the military?
4. How do you handle difficulties after leaving the service?
5. What is your purpose today? How do you know what your purpose is?
6. How does your current purpose affect how you live?

13

★ ★ ★

I Don't Fit In

The depth of friendship you get from the military is priceless; deep friendship as a civilian is possible, too, but hard work is necessary.

A final problem for many veterans trying to find their new place in civilian culture is summarized by the common complaint, "I don't fit in." One warrior described his struggle like this:

"One of the biggest losses when I got out was the camaraderie aspect. I missed the boys. That was really hard. I didn't think it was going to be that hard, honestly. Getting out and waking up in the morning and just being in my own little apartment and being like, what am I going to do right now? *Well, I guess I'm going to go drink some beer and play some video games.*

"I tried to reconnect with my buddy who lives in Massachusetts and another one who lives in Washington and a third one who lives in New Mexico. We tried to get online at the same time and talk for a little bit and play some video games. It sucked because it wasn't the same.

"Another part of this struggle was getting integrated back in with 'the cattle' [civilians]. That sucked, just knowing, *I'm better than you. I know I'm better than you.* I actually got fired because I said that to somebody. My boss was overweight at the factory I worked at and he was giving me crap one time because I was late for work when my step-kids had to do something. And he said to me 'You need to be more responsible.' The Marine Corps thing kicked in hardcore and I'm like, 'You need to responsible, you're fat. You're telling me to be responsible and you're nasty.' He told me, 'You're fired.'"

"I had to try not to do the whole NCO thing to people all the time. These were big issues for me."

When I left the military, I also had a strong feeling of "not fitting in" with civilian life. I struggled to find an appropriate peer group. I went directly to college at age twenty-six, when most other students were eighteen or nineteen years old. I didn't feel as though I fit in. I thought this was due primarily to the maturity gap, as well as my feeling of inadequacy regarding academic proficiency. It turned out I had not quite understood the real issues.

As I continued my college studies and my academic proficiency increased, I also started finding some peers at my maturity level. Still, that feeling of "not fitting in" persisted.

Over time, I recognized that the good friendships I developed were mostly with other veterans. I had prided myself on not excluding new friends simply because they weren't veterans, but I started noticing that we veterans had a like-mindedness and a similar mentality that drew us together.

The conditioning all of us went through had created a way of thinking and perceiving life that gave us a common perspective, even if we had not served together as warriors. We enjoyed a sense of feeling understood, on multiple levels. We felt relieved and affirmed that no one took offense at our dark or off-color humor.

I also found that hanging around others who came from the same warrior culture reminded me of the heights of my identity. In some ways, they helped it to keep going. I do not believe that veterans should not avoid making friends of other veterans out of fear that such friendships might keep them stuck. In fact, veteran friends can be a critical component in the process of moving forward. It becomes a detriment only if a warrior chooses to spend time exclusively with other veterans.

Earlier we considered immigrants who separate themselves from the American culture, surrounding themselves exclusively with vestiges and reminders of their former culture elsewhere. They rarely, if ever, reach out to interact or build friendships with anyone outside of their familiar bubble. They never assimilate into the culture of their new homeland; it's as if they try to convince themselves that they never left the old country.

> The goal of a veteran is not to assimilate, to forget, or abandon a culture so highly valued. If we try to do away with our past culture, we often lose important aspects of the tremendous strength built into our identity as warriors

I do not at all mean that veterans should try to forget the military culture that gave them so much. I believe they should continue to honor that culture through some regular practices, even as they work to form their new identity and adopt new cultural practices in their post-military life. The goal of a veteran is not to assimilate, to forget, or abandon a culture so highly valued. If we try to do away with our past culture, we often lose important aspects of the tremendous strength built into our identity as warriors.

Help for Fitting In

When I help veterans to readjust to civilian culture, I often give them an assignment: make some civilian friends. Of course, they should find friends with whom they get along, who have similar interests and outlooks. "Try to see and appreciate the perspective of your new civilian friends," I tell them. "Over time, you'll begin to see that some good similarities exist that can help you to begin readjusting to the civilian environment."

If a veteran has trouble finding civilian friends, I encourage him or her to get involved in an activity or club that interests them. Mutually enjoyed activities tend to facilitate good friendships. One warrior client joined a rugby club and made great friends there. Some guys make friends through video gaming, although such a solitary activity can have a significant downside: rather than making friends face to face, the friends are essentially virtual. Although the mutually enjoyed activity can help veterans battle the feeling of not fitting in, the isolation of digital game play can make matters worse.

Most veterans struggle with the loss of camaraderie and military friendships when they attempt to re-enter the civilian environment. They go from spending almost twenty-four hours a day with one another, suffering together, and in the case of combat, enduring together significant life-impacting events, to feeling on their own. Military service creates a tremendous bond among warriors that seldom can be wholly replaced.

Those bonds, however, usually were forced. Warriors were forced to interact with other groups of warriors. After they leave the military and enter academic or workplace environments, their interactions are forced only to the point of work projects or school requirements. Many veterans make little effort to move past these interactions because of the frustration they feel with the nature of these exchanges.

My years of clinical experience assure me that when a warrior is assigned a group project at school or work, he will feel great aggravation with other students or co-workers. Often the problem lies with the very different ways the two cultures have been taught to handle group projects. The cultural clash that typically occurs causes veterans to conclude that they cannot get along with civilians. The result stalls the veteran's adaptation to civilian culture. One former combat Marine gave his opinion of group projects:

"I can't stand group projects in school. We all come up with a plan of what we would follow through on; and then when the deadline comes, there's always one person who will not turn in their finished portion. And, of course, there's always one who will turn it in, but you can tell they gave absolutely no effort to doing it the right way. And then I end up having to do that portion of the group member's assigned task. It's like these people have no drive toward mission accomplishment."

I see it repeatedly. Many veterans have tremendous difficulties in making new civilian friends, which makes it hard for them to re-adapt to the civilian environment. They must not forget that community and friendships provide a crucial foundation for building personal resilience. When veterans miss out on community, friendships, and camaraderie, they make it exponentially more difficult for themselves to develop resilience and to adapt.

Try Spiritual Practices

One common practice often helps veterans to more effectively make the transition and thus adapt much easier. Resilience literature makes it clear

that those with significant religious practices can make the adaptation much better
than those who lack them.

Research by the Rand Corporation has
identified spiritual practices as a key issue
and important asset. Their studies identified both risk factors and strength factors
of veterans attempting to transition back to
the civilian world. The research concluded
that the top factor in a warrior's ease of transition is the presence of a robust
spiritual practice.

> "Resilience literature
> makes it clear that those
> with significant religious
> practices can make the
> adaptation much better than
> those who lack them"

Why should a robust spiritual practice make it easier for veterans to make
this transition? Several factors help to explain this conclusion, and many of
them involve community and friendship.

A faith-based community often creates a like-mindedness as well as
many opportunities to relate with others. Spiritual practices bridge the gap
of barriers created by background or history differences through providing a
common viewpoint and perspective. Face-to-face activities often create opportunities for communal support and the building of friendships. Serving
something bigger than yourself is another parallel—how can you get bigger
than God? I could cite many other reasons explaining why spiritual practices
rank at the top among components that ease a warrior's transition into the
civilian environment, but I'll stop here.

I often tell veterans who ask how they can make their transition smooth-
er, "Get spiritual." I explain to them the research that indicates spiritual practices consistently land at the top of ways that help veterans readjust to the
civilian environment. Such practices give veterans a venue in which to "fit
in."

Put Yourself Out There

Please don't miss this element. So many warriors leave the military, lament-
ing over the loss of camaraderie and friendship, only to doom themselves by
feeling that they will never have it again. They cast themselves to the dismal
fate that they will never get it back.

At some level, of course, their statement may be true; but it will damn sure turn out to be true if they don't put themselves out there and make efforts to find and build camaraderie in the civilian world.

Warriors and veterans, you must choose to "fit in" by finding a community (or communities) where you can feel at home, and then working to build friendships and camaraderie there. None of this will "just happen," like it did in the warrior culture. You need to find that hill and take it.

Pass and Review

- factor that causes warriors to feel as though they do not fit in the civilian culture.
- Making intentional efforts to find friends must become the new normal.
- If you don't work at this effort, you will find yourself feeling isolated.
- Practicing faith is a key avenue for warriors to find like-minded friends.

Inspection:

1. Where have you felt as though you didn't fit in, either with the peer group you are in or even with your old peer group?
2. What intentional efforts have you made to make civilian friends? If you haven't made such efforts, why not? What is keeping you from doing this?
3. Do you practice some type of faith? If not, what is keeping you from accessing this resource?
4. Rate yourself on the following scale regarding the effort you are putting forth to create friendships in the civilian world. Explain your rating.

1	2	3	4	5	6	7
No effort	Little effort	Moderate effort		Significant effort		Total effort

14

The Simple Life of Combat

Combat was a summit in your life, but you cannot stay there.
You must find a new summit.

Civilians typically express surprise when they hear of two common complaints I often get from veterans during therapy sessions.

"I wish I was back in combat," many veterans tell me.

"I wish I would've died in combat instead of coming home," others say.

Most civilians see war as hell, and they can't imagine why anyone would want to go back to *that*. Yes, war is a place of traumatic experiences and regular moral dilemmas. But another component of war fulfills the warrior. Warriors who go to war get to fulfill their primary purpose, which can be deeply fulfilling.

When I say "fulfilling," don't think "enjoyable." Fulfillment and enjoyment are not close to being the same thing. When many warriors leave the military and re-enter the civilian world, they often express fond memories and admiration for their combat experience, not because they are sociopaths, but for all the positive things that culminated in that experience.

They remember the closeness of their bond, the sacrifices they made for each other, the rush of bullets whistling past them, the satisfaction of winning a hard and dangerous fight. Combat can be the most significant experience that individuals ever have in their entire lives.

> Many warriors consider combat much easier to accept than civilian life

But whatever the causes of this warm sentiment toward combat and serving in the military, it reveals a very common struggle for warriors trying to re-enter a civilian environment. They deeply miss their former lives as warriors. Many of them consider combat much easier to accept than civilian life.

Get Me Back to Combat, *Please!*

I have worked with countless veterans who, a few short years after leaving the military, have a change of heart about their decision to get out. They had really looked forward to the civilian life, where they would not be told what to do, where they could become the master of their own destiny, and where they could use the tremendous skills and valuable experiences they had gained in the military to become highly successful civilians.

Or so they thought.

After experiencing many of the difficulties of the readjustment, they try to get back into military service or contract for para-military organizations. Many warriors have returned to Iraq or Afghanistan as contractors. This desire to willingly put oneself in harm's way again often baffles civilians.

I once worked with a former Marine who was diagnosed with PTSD and put on medication. He worked for years to get off his prescription drugs and reduce his PTSD to the point where he could get a letter stating it had ceased to be a problem. He then promptly joined another military service so he could return to combat.

Why would warriors want to go back to combat? In this final chapter, I will focus on one last key factor that troubles many warriors trying to re-enter the civilian world.

Civilian Life Is Too Complicated

Although combat is high risk and often full of trauma, there is a clear simplicity to it. Combat vets commonly speak of the simplicity of a warrior's life, day in and day out. When we send our warriors to war, we have many methods of helping warriors to offload home responsibilities so that they can clearly focus on the mission at hand.

They can put loans on hold while deployed. Their family usually tries to shelter them from difficult scenarios taking place at home. They sign over the power of attorney so family members can take care of the bills and other responsibilities that the warrior normally would handle. They receive psychological permission to not focus or worry about things in the civilian world. These are all important things to accomplish so the warrior can completely focus on the task at hand.

When warriors leave the military and lose many of the support components designed to help them focus on the mission, it can feel overwhelming. Many veterans have a tough time balancing dozens of civilian responsibilities. It's not that they're incapable of handling these duties, but rather that they're laser focused on living with a singular focus and purpose. When they leave the military, this singular focus and purpose gets crowded out by many seemingly trivial responsibilities. Many want to re-enter the military so they can return to war and the simplicity it offers.

The complexity of multiple responsibilities can feel aggravating, especially when the task feels inconsequential after a life and death combat deployment. Sheltering warriors from the general responsibilities of civilian life results in the feeling that such tasks are trivial or meaningless, which can create even more frustration. Many times, the outcome can be a longing to go back to "the simple life."

A Structure Established in Adulthood

The lives of military personnel are driven and directed for just one purpose, and they receive the support they need to be fully committed to that purpose. Young soldiers, sailors, airmen, or Marines never have to worry about their housing or the bills and responsibilities that come with it. Nor do they have to worry about their food or where it comes from. Many of the components basic to civilian adulthood are taken care of so that the warrior can focus on his or her mission. Such treatment does not make warriors feel as though they are not yet adults; quite the opposite, it makes them feel as though they are above civilian adults.

Although warriors learn this form of adulthood in a military structure, it continues to influence them once they return to the civilian world. It comes as a shock to the warrior's system to learn how to be a responsible adult in the civilian world. Let's look more closely at one of the most significant areas that tend to create difficult issues for warriors and their families.

The money dilemma

Money mismanagement creates significant problems for many veterans. Providing many basics for warriors so they can focus on their mission tends to create a safety net for money mismanagement. For the first time in their lives, many young warriors are getting a paycheck and living away from home. The military provides all their fundamental needs of life, and for the most part, their living affairs are directed for them. This creates a low consequence scenario for service members to go out and spend all their money.

My first duty station was in Kaneohe Bay, Hawaii. Young infantrymen stationed there commonly went out on the town on the first and the fifteenth day of the month and spent their whole paycheck over the weekend. The opposite of payday weekends they ate at the chow hall and stayed in their rooms. They faced few consequences for spending their whole paycheck on frivolous things. All our basic needs were still covered.

The unfortunate consequence for young warriors who do a single enlistment and then get out of the military (the norm) is that they develop spending habits that create substantial difficulty for them once they re-enter the civilian world. I have worked with many veterans who create significant problems for themselves because they do not know how to manage their money. Untold numbers of spouses and couples in therapy have complained about a service member's mismanagement of money.

Moreover, when a career military person gets out with their family, it is not fully understood how it will affect the underlying security they feel. Many career military personnel get out and have mental breakdowns, not because of PTSD, but because of the stress of trying to find a civilian job that can provide a level of security similar to what they enjoyed in the military. This process usually takes years, and the family often feels the turbulence of this struggle.

This doesn't mean that *every* military person has trouble with money. I know plenty of warriors who handle their money very well. But it does emphasize that money management is a very common struggle among veterans. This is another reason why many warriors want to return to combat. In combat, you do not have to worry about bills or other financial responsibilities. You often watch your bank account grow because of your combat pay and tax-free income.

It's standard practice for me to begin with veterans or couples to ask about their financial situation. I have multiple referral sources that can help them to learn better money management.

Problems of money mismanagement do not mean that warriors have failed to become adults. Our country created this scenario so that our warriors could focus on war fighting. This is a natural consequence of using these men and women in this way.

Something's Missing Deep in the Soul

Multiple factors influence a warrior's desire to return to combat. These factors do not imply that the warrior is broken, nor do they suggest that veterans can operate effectively only in the theater of war. These conditions were built into the warrior and are natural outcomes of walking the warrior path.

When veterans return to a civilian environment, these issues often create difficulties for them. They are not pathologies. We made these warriors this way, we asked them to be this for us, and now we must work to understand why so many veterans find it so difficult to assimilate back into the civilian environment. Some warriors find it more appealing to return to a dangerous but fulling scenario. They would rather feel uncomfortable than not valued.

> We made these warriors this way, we asked them to be this for us, and now we must work to understand why so many veterans find it so difficult to assimilate back into the civilian environment.

Pass and Review

- Combat is usually one of the most significant events that has taken place in the life of a warrior. Not much compares to the good and bad they experience there.
- After warriors leave the military, it can shock them to realize all they have lost.
- Warriors go from a singular, significance-focused life, to (what seems to them) a trivial, plurality of responsibilities life.

- Money mismanagement is a common problem for many veterans.

Inspection

1. What would you list as the most significant experiences of your life? What are your top five?
2. Have you ever thought, *Life would be easier if I could just go back in the military?* Explain.
3. Described the burden you may feel of the seemingly trivial responsibilities you must handle in the civilian world. What responsibilities may feel trivial to you but still demand your attention?
4. What has been the most difficult thing for you to manage since you have gotten out?

★ ★ ★

Warriors as Assets: Re...Cover!

Warriors who adapt their skills, abilities, and experiences
to the civilian world have unlimited potential for success.
But warriors who do not adapt will run into one barrier after another.

Many warriors run into great difficulty when they try to return to the civilian world. Does that mean they are permanently damaged or broken? Far from it!

The tremendous number of skillsets and abilities instilled into every warrior make them highly valuable commodities for any employer. Veterans transitioning back into the civilian world may need some help to make that transition, but they have amazing potential just waiting to be tapped.

Many smart organizations have seen this staggering potential and are making intentional efforts to help veterans adapt to their new reality. Other organizations see the potential in veterans, but do not know how to properly tap their full capacity or help them transition to a civilian work culture. Without question, the organizations that employ these warriors and give them the skills to adapt create great organizational assets.

Warriors as Force Multipliers

Warriors who re-enter the civilian world are force multipliers. In the military context, a force multiplier refers to something that gives a unit a greater advantage, thus compounding the effectiveness of the unit.

Adding a crew-served weapon, for example, provides a force multiplier. It takes a gun team to effectively operate a belt-fed machine gun. In combat, a crew-served weapon can give a unit tremendous strategic advantage when it is properly placed and manned. With just a few men, you can cover a great area of distance and breadth on a battlefield. If a commander does not know how to properly use a crew-served weapon, however, he can diminish its value to the mission and frustrate his weapons team. Both lose in the scenario. Such a commander does not maximize the effective capability available to him.

> When you employ warriors carefully conditioned for war fighting in the most extreme circumstances, and you properly train those warriors to work effectively within your organization, you have tremendous employees with built-in leadership traits and training.

The principle is clear. When you employ warriors carefully conditioned for war fighting in the most extreme circumstances, *and* you properly train those warriors to work effectively within your organization, you have tremendous employees with built-in leadership traits and training. They also bring multiple traits that greatly benefit any organization, such as teamwork and mission focus.

Will it take a little extra time and attention to fully maximize the capabilities of these veterans? Perhaps. But if you want better, deeper, and longer lasting results, you'll make the little extra effort required. Imagine what your organization could do with several force multipliers in the right spots!

The Turtle and the Hare

To describe the advantages of hiring veterans, I often use the metaphor of the turtle and the hare. Using their skills and experience, warriors will catch up with and eventually pass those who lack such valuable military experience.

I often work with young warriors who did a single enlistment in the military, got out, and then immediately enrolled in college. These young warriors initially tend to feel tremendous frustration in the new academic environment. Much of their frustration comes from being surrounded by eighteen-year-olds who begin school with a much more streamlined expectation of what happens in college. Most of these young warriors took a minimum of four years off from school before returning to a very different environment.

Their frustration is compounded by combat deployments, because they have experienced a very different style of life than their fellow students, along with a different set of priorities. Quite often their opinions are not politically correct for an academic environment, nor are they valued.

I work with these veterans by coaching and encouraging them. I often remind them of the tortoise and the hare. The tortoise starts out slow but stays consistent and methodical and eventually passes the hare.

Warriors transitioning back to civilian life are much like the tortoise because they must first learn how to navigate the college academic environment. This often feels to them like a delayed start. Many of the aptitudes required in college are proficiency skills; once you get out of practice, these skills begin to diminish and must be re-learned. The students who go straight from high school to college essentially take no break in this proficiency and usually have little trouble meeting the criteria for a college environment. The young warrior, however, must do some catch-up work to get back up to speed.

I've seen this scenario play out especially in math classes at community colleges. Many times, these young warriors get enrolled in below-college-level math classes so they can catch up to the collegiate level. Their classes often last for the duration of their associate degree. To say the least, returning warriors feel great frustration in math.

To successfully navigate this challenge, these young warriors must grasp that they will have to adapt for the civilian environment most of what they learned in the military. If they do not adapt, they either conclude that the instilled military traits do not work or they continue to pound a square peg into a round hole—in the process damaging both those around them and themselves.

We do not leave this frustration there; we work with it. These young warriors feel greatly encouraged once they regain their proficiency and then add the qualities that the military instilled in them. These skills eventually begin to compound their efforts.

The tortoise and the hare metaphor breaks down right here, because when these young warriors become proficient again, you see a heightened level of proficiency that makes them *more* effective than the younger students. In effect, the tortoise becomes a super-hare.

I experienced this phenomenon myself as I moved from undergraduate to graduate school. As I continued the path and became more proficient, my ability to comprehend and apply content began to exceed that of my civilian peers. As my competency grew, I found myself working with clients far more complex than those who worked with my civilian peers.

Here's the point: while it may take time and effort for the veteran's skill sets to adapt to the civilian environment, once they do, the warrior's growth curve far exceeds that of a civilian peer group.

Making the Final About Face

Hear me on this, "You are not broken unless you choose to be."

You are what the warrior culture made you to be; now it is time to become what your employer, spouse, children, and *you* need to you to be.

> You are what the warrior culture made you to be; now it is time to become what your employer, spouse, children, and you need to you to be

Remember that you cannot make the final about face alone. Although you will have to do much of the work on your own, you must gather a tribe around you so that together you can all push one another to keep going.

As you finish this book, I want you to remember that it took thousands of hours and millions of dollars to make you into a warrior. All that work will not be undone simply because you're out of the military. I also want you to know that you are not alone in your struggle. Many of the struggles you're going through are completely normal.

Although I've done my best to give you some practical help, recognize that it's just a start. A lot of intentional conditioning went in to make you what you are, so don't hesitate to reach out for assistance. A multitude of organizations and people want to help you make this transition. Reaching out for help does not mean you're broken; in fact, reaching out for help is often the most potent preventive measure that keeps you from becoming broken.

A Final Word

I do not claim to be the expert in all things and I know that I could be misunderstood in many ways regarding the issues I address in this book. But one thing is certain: I've seen far too many warriors struggle, give up, or even self-destruct after leaving the military. I would be remiss to make no attempt to help those heading toward a very kinetic AO (area of operation) without giving them the proper warning.

Too many warriors have worked hard on their alleged problem (PTSD), only to continue struggling after finishing treatment. Why do they still struggle? They do so because their problem goes much deeper than PTSD.

I hope you now understand at a higher level the depth of the struggle involved with transitioning from the military to civilian life. I also hope the practical steps I've provided can begin to help you get out of that struggle. By intentionally focusing your efforts on a successful transition, you *will* move through this deep valley and reach another summit.

May the view from there be glorious, just as I'm sure it will be for the veteran who told me the following. I leave you with his words:

"I have leadership and I have determination. But I think the greatest asset I have is determination, just like in the Marine Corps.

At every rank, you've got to ask, 'Okay, how do I get to the next line? What will prepare me to be successful?' But for me, it wasn't just about obtaining the next rank. So, I worked very hard. I paid attention to what I needed to build a toolbox that would prepare me to succeed. I'm going to do the same thing in the civilian world, whatever job I go into.

If it's an entry-level position, I'm willing to take an entry-level position. If I can see upward trajectory and a position within that company that I would want to excel at, that would be beneficial both for myself and for the company, that's what I'm going to do. The same thing I did in the Marine Corps: "Here's what I want. Here's where I want to be. How do I get there?" And then work hard and get there.

Tools for the Transition

For the warrior, classroom time is only the first step;
now it is time for Prac App.

I have written most of this book so that you can better understand what you are going through. That has been your classroom time—an important area—but now you must do the Prac App.

This section is designed to help you apply the content in a practical way. As we all know, classroom time means nothing if you are not willing to apply it. To start all of these may not directly apply to you, but at least one of these tools will apply to every veteran. Use what you need to help you. I have used all of these with warriors that have successfully made the transition back to the civilian environment.

Whenever we did PT and performed some type of exercise, we would get to the point where we'd have to get up from completing the exercise, stand at attention, and wait for the one leading the exercise to hear the command, "Re…cover!"

This is that time.

Fundamental: The Adaptation Mindset

By the time I got out of the Marine Corps, I had developed a tremendous skill set perfect for military use. Many of those skills, however, did not translate directly over to the civilian world. Even if I was learning the unfamiliar "civilian language" relevant to one area or another, I had to take each skill or competence into my heart and find fresh ways to apply them to my new setting. In other words, I had to adapt my experience and training for different use in my new, civilian role.

Once I learned this, I was able to excel beyond my peers because I took my years of training and guided them into a new application and arena. I focused on adaptation, not assimilation or restoration.

Transitions: Walking Through the Process of Change

In his book *Transition,* Jerry Bridges helps us to understand some critical areas of life change. Fundamentally, life always involves a change of status. Change will always happen. How we deal with change will determine if it helps us or harms us.

Bridges emphasizes that change and transition are not the same thing. Just because you leave the military, then, does not mean that you will transition in a healthy way. Change is circumstantial and behavioral, whereas transition is more psychological.

One day, you *will* find yourself out of the military (if you're not out already). That change will occur or has already taken place, whether you like it or not. Even so, you may not have *psychologically* transitioned out of the military. Throughout my years of counseling I've heard story after story in which veterans in their first few months or years after getting out of the military lost jobs, relationships, and even their freedom. Why? Because they acted in ways appropriate to their former active-duty lives but highly inappropriate for their current civilian lives.

The main purpose of this book has been to help you understand the enormous power of the conditioning that warriors go through, so that you can grasp how difficult the psychological transition will be to civilian life. We start the application process, then, by helping *you* to understand that you need to take the initiative and make the effort to psychologically transition.

Sometimes the transition can take place naturally, with time and acclimatization, but many times the transition never fully takes place because the veteran didn't take the initiative to make it happen. Why not try to avoid unnecessary losses during your time of transition when you're already dealing with so many other areas of loss?

I won't repeat what Bridges covers so well. I will encourage you, after you finish this book and complete some of the tests given, to read his book. I believe it will help you to understand in more detail some key steps to a successful transition. Here I will briefly outline the steps that Bridges suggests.

1. Accept the endings.

I know this may sound silly, but I also know that just because you're no longer in the military does not mean that you've truly accepted your departure, along with all the losses that go with it. You need to accept the loss of certain aspects of your former military lifestyle. And remember, it *was* a lifestyle, not merely a job.

Bridges states, "To become something else, you have to stop being what you are now; to start doing things a new way, you have to end the way you are doing them now; and to develop a new attitude or outlook, you have to let go of the old one you have now. Even though it sounds backwards, endings always come first."

Here's the first question to ask yourself: "As my last season of life has come to an end, what do I have to accept now about that reality?" I know this seems like an overly simplistic question, but you truly must be able to answer it if you are going to free yourself to move forward. Remember, you want to keep yourself from either living too much in the past or from losing the value of your past, just because you don't know how to bring it forward. This process starts with you identifying the things you must accept as over.

I hate to break it to you, but for many of us, training for war has come to an end. You must accept that fact.

I remember truly missing the feel of an M4 in my shoe shoulder and feeling the recoil as I put rounds on target. Of course, right now I could get an M4 and put rounds on target, but my purpose and mission in doing so would be very different from when I was still on active duty in the Corps. Then it was a mission; now it would be a novelty.

I know that many veterans go into law enforcement or back into the military or join a paramilitary organization, and for them this may be a reality. But the vast majority of us will re-enter the civilian world. Before we can move forward, we have to accept that our active-duty season has ended.

If you have not yet done this simple task, it is time.

Get a blank piece of paper and make three categories. The first category includes things that will end once you're out of the military. Think of everything you can, from the large components to the simplest little things. In the third category, write out all the things that you believe will directly apply to the civilian world, with little to no change. This list will be much shorter than the first one.

The second category, the middle column, will list all the highly valuable items that must be adapted to fit into your new civilian context. This middle column really reflects a new mindset you must develop so you can begin evaluating your experiences and seeing how they fit into various scenarios where you may need them. This middle column will probably end up being the longest of the three.

Your military experience has significant value in many areas of life, but because the military culture and the civilian culture differ so radically, much of your military experience does not directly apply. It must be adapted.

You probably will need to make your middle list an ongoing project, because many things you don't at first think of will need to be adapted for your new scenario/career. Make sure, however, that you do not lose the value of any skill set you have and the value it will bring to a new setting, once adapted.

One former reconnaissance Marine took up surfing after he got out of the military and had a significant learning curve, to the point where he began surfing better than many others who had surfed for many years. "Once I realized that surfing was really about learning to read the waves," he said, "and I learned that this is usually what take years of experience to get better, I was able to adapt the skills I got from being a recon Marine, doing hours of beach observation and wave surveys for amphibious landings. My trained skillset gave me a baseline to make great use of. I did not even realize how valuable of a skill this would be in my life after the military."

2. Understand the neutral zone.

The neutral zone is what you experience once you get out of the military. Of course, there's a honeymoon. You get excited because you don't have to wear fatigues any longer or do zero 530 PT. After all that wears off, however, you begin to feel those losses and start having the struggles that normally accompany culture shock

You feel the insecurity of financially providing, often from very unstable jobs. Or you feel the frustration of going to school with people half your age and a small fraction of your life experience. Now you're in the neutral zone. It feels very uncomfortable to be in the neutral zone, to be frank. *But it's meant to be.*

Can you imagine going into boot camp and just staying in boot camp? You'd be like many of those poor bastards who got recycled through boot camp multiple times because of medical injuries. We all think of boot camp like a type of purgatory. The reality is that it's a neutral zone. You're leaving the world of civilians and entering the world of warriors. You're in the in between, where it can feel very uncomfortable. But at least we knew it would last only two or three months!

When you enter the civilian world, the neutral zone can feel like no man's land where you cannot see the ending. This is especially true if you're getting out of the military and going to school, because school essentially places you in the neutral zone for multiple years.

You should expect that it's going to be difficult. While you're in the neutral zone, trying to figure out your next step, things will seem hard. Bridges' book *Transitions* will walk you through many more details in this area and will give you some tangible things to do to mitigate the difficulty.

For now, accept that the struggles you will face for the next period of your life will come and go as you adapt to your new environment. This area for acceptance can be difficult because you will go through many unknown areas. You must accept the uncertainty and know that it is part of the process of transition. If you fight against this or move through it too quickly, you may rush into an unsuitable job or career or education track. What happens then? You'll hate it and will have to go through yet another difficult transition.

Just ask many of the vets you know. Most will tell you that you need to pause and figure out this part. Most of us do not figure it out while we are still in, but we need to get money quickly after we get out. We then rush into a career that we don't really need or want.

As we transition, we typically must do a lot of acceptance. Acceptance is not giving in but rather properly understanding the situation's reality and letting this new understanding reorient our perception of the situation. As we all know, this is a critical step on the battlefield. You must be able to assess the situation, and even if it doesn't go according to plan, you accept that reality and make whatever changes must be made. You invite disaster if you try to fight for the plan despite the reality.

Let me give you a tip regarding how to help your mind accept difficult things. First, catch yourself whenever you try to hold onto what you must let go. Accept the new reality. Whenever you start reminiscing over the way things used to be, for example, catch yourself. Then challenge yourself. Say something like, "That was a good season of life, but that is over now." Just saying this to yourself will not make the change, of course, but once you have reminded yourself of this truth multiple times, it begins to settle into the psyche.

Remember, purpose and identity abhor a vacuum. If you are in the neutral zone and you do not put anything into these areas, you'll naturally gravitate back toward the old, strong identities. Alternatively, you will find yourself drawn toward identities and purposes that have no power to truly fulfill you.

3. The new beginning.

Here you identify your new normal. This is the place where you start to identify your new purpose and what identity will fill that purpose. Many veterans get stuck in the neutral zone because they cannot find that meaningful new purpose and identity. This explains why we will address the next tangible things you can do that will help you to identify your new beginning and so help you to get through the neutral zone.

One warrior who went through many difficulties gives this advice:

> You need to buckle down, use the discipline that you got from the military and plan a path. You can't just sit in your fighting hole and think it is all going to work out. You gotta be proactive. You gotta go on the assault. You can't be defensive. If you don't do this, life will bite you in the ass.

The first and often most difficult area is figuring out your new identity, so let's start there.

Find Your New Code

Identity is a complex and daunting concept to tackle. A whole book dedicated to that topic could not cover all the bases. And God forbid you've taken any philosophy classes, because most will only muddy your understanding of identity.

Thankfully, with our warrior experience we have something powerful going for us. We have experienced what a powerful identity truly is. Most of us have lived out that identity.

After we leave the military, however, we can't fully live out the identity given to us; it must be transitioned. Still, while that must happen, we do *not* want to lose the values that are critically important to that identity. Since we must start somewhere, what better place to begin than where the military started in its conditioning of our identity? Remember that we are not trying to replace that identity, but to adapt it to the new civilian scenario. We want to take the applicable things for the new culture and set aside the things not applicable.

We start by establishing our value system. You can do this just as it happened in the military, through identifying your personal creed/code. Remember how our value systems provide the foundations that establish our identity? Our value systems in the military came from our codes and creeds.

Step One

Find the creed that most impacted you, the one that you most identified with. Once you find that creed, print it out. If you already have it memorized, write it out on a piece of paper.

Step Two

Take that creed and honestly evaluate which sections of it no longer fit within the civilian culture that you have experienced or anticipate experiencing. If you have a hard time with this, try to interact with other veterans who already have made the transition, or perhaps with another civilian you trust who can give you insight.

When you identify these things that no longer fit your current scenario, cross them out. At the same time, make sure that you're not being too hasty. Don't eliminate some principle that would still apply in a different way to your new setting.

Step Three

Identify in your creed the things that you truly want to bring forward into your life. Sometimes they can be great principles surrounded by context that no longer fits your new culture. Identify the principle and circle it as something important that you want to adapt.

Step Four

On another page, rewrite the creed without the excluded areas and add the circled areas. At this point you may have to add phrasing that applies to your new civilian life. If your old creed said, "Never leave a fallen comrade behind," for example, you might adapt it to, "have a sacrificial mentality toward friendships and relationships." Don't be afraid to brainstorm here! Put the creed in your own words. Make it work for your own life. Even if it doesn't seem to fit your current life, include it if it reflects what you want your identity to become.

Remember, identity is not only descriptive, but prescriptive. Even if the creed does not currently describe you, if it describes what you want to become, it can have just as powerful an effect on your identity.

Consider, for example, the well-known "leaders code" which Marine leaders had to take to heart (and many of us wish that leaders in the civilian world would take to heart).

The Leaders Code

"I become a leader by what I do. I know my strengths and my weaknesses, and I strive constantly for self-improvement. I live by a moral code with which I set an example for others to emulate. I know my job and I carry out the spirit as well as the letter of the orders I received. I take the initiative and seek responsibilities, and I face situations with boldness and confidence. I estimate the situation and make my own decisions as to the best course of action. No matter what the requirements, I stay with the job until the job is done; no matter what the results, I assume full responsibility. I train my men as a team and lead them with tact, with enthusiasm, and with justice. I command their confidence and their loyalty: they understand their orders, and I follow through energetically to ensure that their duties are fully discharged. I keep my men informed and I make their welfare one of my primary concerns. These things I do selflessly in fulfillment of their obligations of leadership and for their treatment of the group goal."

Notice the creed's continual references to "I." You can also use "I will" statements. Don't get too caught up in the structure as much as you truly personalize some of the content.

Consider what one veteran did with the leadership code and how he personalized it to his own experience and walk of life:

Personalized Code
(example from a veteran)

I am a husband, father, leader by what I do.

I know my strengths and my weaknesses, and I strive constantly for self-improvement with self-mastery.

I live by this code, with which I set an example for others to emulate. I know my role and my calling and I carry out the spirit of what God has directed me to do.

I take the initiative and seek responsibility, and I face situations with boldness and confidence in God's greater purpose.

I estimate the situation and make prayerful decisions as to the best course of action. No matter what the consequences, I hold to my integrity and honor; no matter what the results, I assume full responsibility for my actions.

I train my family as a team and lead them with tact, with enthusiasm, and with justice. I command their confidence and their loyalty; they understand my love for them, and I follow through energetically to ensure that they are fully equipped to serve the King.

I keep my family in prayer and I make their spiritual and physical welfare one of my primary concerns.

These things I do selflessly with humility in fulfillment of the privilege of leadership that God has bestowed on me.

I will always keep my mission clear and present.

Your own creed will take some time and effort to develop and even more time and effort to install in your life and actions. If you truly mean it, it will impact your identity. You must ingest it into your soul on your own, because no one will force this on you.

It would be a good to post it in a place where you often see it. One reason why our military creeds had so much impact was that we truly valued them and what they represented. Now you must create a creed that you personally value, because the culture around you will not instill these things in you.

Memorize it! Memorization has a powerful impact on how the brain absorbs content. In the military, superiors always tried to get us to memorize things, especially creeds and codes. At first, I thought this was just brainwashing, but I have learned through neuropsychology and neurobiology that when your brain memorizes something, the action builds physical structures in the brain that create patterns of thinking. Memorizing something and regurgitating it, over and over again, has a powerful effect on a person. I will not bore you with the details of the neuropsychology, but trust me, there is great power in memorizing. If you want to become more like some creed that you admire, then memorize it, repeat it, and your actions will build a new structure in your brain to help you live out that creed.

Doing this creates a sound foundation for your identity. While this will not completely establish a revised identity, it is foundational. This is the place to start.

Remember, identity abhors a vacuum. You cannot live without an identity, and if you do not establish a new identity, you will gravitate back toward your old identity—and if it's not active, it will only depress you.

Now, let's move on to establishing a personal purpose. The great thing about establishing a personal purpose is that it overlaps identity. These two elements should feed into one another.

Set Your New Mission/Purpose

Once you have lived with a clear purpose and mission and felt the personal fulfillment that those things bring, you will not be able to tolerate living with an obscured or unclear life direction. You may be able to get by for a little while, but soon you will feel the growing chasm in your soul that remains unfulfilled.

You need to find your new purpose!

Your purpose will change and remain somewhat fluid as you change, but it will always move in the same basic direction that fits you and your needs.

I've worked with many veterans who got out and immediately started chasing self-gain and advancement. I'll tell you now that such a "purpose" will ultimately leave you empty. After years of making big money, warriors often still reminisce about being selfless and serving something bigger than themselves.

Finding your purpose can be a difficult process, but this is not new to you. To be a warrior and to acquire that strong purpose that drove you, you had to go through great difficulty. The difference now is that it will not be as physically difficult as it will be mentally and emotionally difficult. Many will not have the fortitude or strength to push themselves past the difficulty, but if you don't, you will end up wondering about your own life, *What's the point?*

So, where do you start in finding a personal purpose? Let me help you begin.

Purpose Is Your "Why"

Your purpose gives you the "why" of your existence, supplying a powerful reason for getting up every morning. I suggest you craft a purpose statement, which has several key characteristics. Let me summarize in outline form how to create your own purpose statement.

1. Characteristics of a Purpose Statement
   a. The purpose statement you're trying to develop is similar to "commander's intent" in an operations order. It's meant to be general with a lot of room to move and take initiative. Make sure, however, to add enough specifics that it gives you a clear direction.
   b. Large umbrella
   c. North Star, directional (vs. destination)
   d. For a lifetime
2. Benefits of a Purpose Statement
   a. Having a clearly defined purpose statement is *freeing*.
      1. You know where you need to go and where you *do not* need to go.
      2. You know what's important and what isn't.
   b. Having a clearly defined purpose statement helps *focus your activity*.
      1. You know *what* should be done and *why*.
   c. Having a clearly defined purpose statement gives you a sense of *direction*.
      1. You have a compass indicating *True North*.
      2. A purpose statement is meant to be a cardinal direction for your life; it is not meant to be a specific azimuth. It should give you general direction and as you walk through terrain, you might have to make specific calls that the cardinal direction will help.
3. How to Write a Purpose Statement
   a. Review and reflect: What in your life has been the most fulfilling?
   b. Ask: Why do I exist?
   c. Probe: Why is that important then. . .?
   d. Focus: Get to the bull's eye of the bullseye.

Now the hard part comes. You must begin writing out your statement. Do not put too much pressure on yourself to get it exactly right the first time.

Think of it at this stage as brainstorming. Allow yourself to be creative and just get things out. A good reference might be to note what others have noticed in you.

If you're struggling to identify some of these things, consider a few tips. Ask people who know you really well to name some words they would use to describe you. Or think back to your greatest accomplishments or times in life when you felt the most fulfilled. Try to categorize those memories into single words that describe you or a quality that you embodied.

If you're still having difficulty, just find one or two words and then look up their synonyms. You'll often find words that better describe you or feel more impactful to you.

Write down ten key words that answer the questions, *why I exist, or what is unique to me.*

1. _____   6. _____

2. _____   7. _____

3. _____   8. _____

4. _____   9. _____

5. _____   10. _____

From this list of ten words, identify the three most significant words that describe you. Choose the words that not only describe you, but also reflect what you want your life to be about. Remember, identity and purpose are not only descriptive but also prescriptive.

To test these words to see if they resonate with you, put them in a "to" statement, as in, "to inspire," "to innovate," "to impact." Whatever these words are, they should be active. Putting them into a "to" statement helps you to see what that word would look like in an active mode.

You've already done a lot of work and thinking about your past. Now consider some specific questions that may help you to identify other nuances.

4. Key Questions to Bring Clarity
   a. How am I unique from any other person in existence? (Consider your situation in life right now: who you are, what you do, what you like/dislike, what you can do that others can't etc.)
   b. What has been my greatest strength in the past?
   c. What is my greatest single strength now?
   d. If I had all the money, skill, and education it took, what would I do?
   e. If I knew I couldn't fail, what would I attempt?
   f. If I were important, what would I be doing?
   g. What need do you see in the world that you feel strongly about? What do you see out there that you believe like somebody should be addressing?
   h. What would I want my headstone to read? Try putting your "to" statement on this and see if it would resonate with how you would like people to remember you after you're gone. If the only thing on your headstone was "to inspire," would that be enough for you? Would that describe a life worth living?
5. Putting It All Together
   a. Write your *primary* identified word from your list of ten. (To _____)

This is the core of who you are. Regardless of the circumstances in your life, you would still do this because it's who you are.

    a. Write in the identified, *need* that you feel drives you. This is the "who."

    b. Write in the "how" of the way you will accomplish this.

    c. Write in the "why." This is where you explain why this is important for you. Your personal Code should influence how you write this.

6. Example of Purpose Statement:

    a. To inspire

    b. those in my sphere of influence,

    c. my teaching, and my writing,

    d. to living a life worth living and honoring the sacrifice of fallen warriors.

My Purpose

Once you have this written out, it's time to test it. Take your working purpose statement and begin to dream about your future. If fifteen or twenty years down the line you were living out this purpose statement, what would your life look like?

Use your imagination and think about all the details of every aspect of your life. What would you be doing for work? What would your family look like? Where would you be living? What would your daily routine look like? Try to truly visualize what all of this would look like. Once you've done this thoroughly, then ask yourself, "Is this really what I would want from my life?"

No doubt, many details will change throughout your life, but this test should help you to determine if this purpose statement is enough to inspire and motivate you.

Many guys I work with have a hard time using their imagination to dream about a personal future. Let's admit it, though; didn't all of us do this when we were going through boot camp? We all dreamed of what our future would be like once we had completed boot camp and could be called a warrior.

Holding to the dream is what usually helps you get through difficulties. The dream also inspires you to make a commitment requiring such sacrifice.

Don't brush this off! Make the effort, force yourself to dream about your future.

If your purpose statement passed this test, just as with the creed, you need to commit it to memory. If this truly is your purpose, then you should memorize it, just as they had us memorize our purpose statements in the military. Memorize your personal purpose and begin to form yourself and your identity around it.

I still remember the purpose statement instilled into me as an infantry Marine: "to locate, close with, and destroy enemy by fire maneuver, and repel enemy's assault by fire and close combat." I memorized this purpose statement and it helped to form who I was as a Marine. Now my purpose statement is: To encourage and make an impact with warriors by leading, counseling, teaching, speaking, and [now] authoring. This is now my North Star that helps me to make decisions for my life, and have a follow on mission that creates purpose. As I now live the civilian life, I have a meaningful purpose, that is just as impactful as my previous mission.

Create a Vision

In the last step of this process, you use your purpose statement and the dream that you took time to visualize to create a vision for your future.

There are many ways to make a vision. Just look up "create a vision" on YouTube to get thousands of ideas. Moreover, we have hundreds of examples of individuals who have reached the highest levels of performance and satisfaction in life by developing a vision that helped them move toward their vision. The famous axiom is true: If you aim at nothing, you'll hit it every time. The point of a vision is to create a target you can aim for.

Your vision can be a short statement that incorporates your purpose statement and your dream of what your future will look like. Or it could be a picture of something that you hang on your wall. Only you truly know what this picture represents, but it continually reminds you of your direction and purpose.

One caution here: A clear purpose and mission can be taken to an extreme. Beware of putting so much focus on the future that you lose sight of the present.

I had one Vietnam vet, age seventy-five, who reflected on his life. "One thing that I have learned," he told me, "is to have a vision in your life for your future, and then to live presently every day, making the most of every day. Then you will achieve that vision."

Too many warriors set their mission and then lose sight of the present, which leads not to fulfillment, but to regret. Make sure you don't look back someday and find that you missed so much in life because you focused so strongly on the future.

Find Your New Tribe: Dealing with Culture Shock

You are no longer in the military culture. I know, it's like losing a family. Yes, you can still keep in touch, but it will never be the same. No one will force you to build camaraderie with others. You are on your own. You must find a new tribe and learn to fit in with its members.

Again, this new normal will take time, effort, energy, and initiative to achieve. Look for a place where you can find like-minded people.

This is where faith often comes in for many warriors. You will not find warriors, but you will be able to find and relate to good people if your faith practice aligns you in the spiritual disciplines. When you find these connections where you can share the struggles you're having as you fight the battle in this new season of life, you'll see that camaraderie will develop over time.

Understand that this area is more organic. You can't often systematically accomplish tangible steps, because developing relationships just doesn't work that way. Developing relationships can be a complex thing.

In the military, we formed relationships through suffering and continual proximity, with all of us moving toward a singular purpose. Not so in the civilian world. We must shift our behavior and expectations and understand that it may take longer to build those friendships. Still, the process must begin somewhere.

I once asked a combat vet, "What helped you make the transition successfully?" He replied, "One of the best things that happened to me was I got into mountain biking. Then every weekend I would begin to hang out with civilians who were doing mountain bike trips. It gave me adrenaline, like being in the military, and a community that we would experience the adrenaline together. Camaraderie came through these trips. I also developed friendships that I found could be very fulfilling because they accepted me without any level of performance. It was very different than coming from the military where performance was part of your acceptance."

This veteran began to find that certain elements of the civilian relationships he developed were better than his military friendships. This helped him to begin to accept the culture that he was trying to re-enter.

Understand that it will take longer now to build satisfying relationships than it did in the military, in part because you will not suffer together as you did in the service. Now you must bring to one another the difficulties you are going through. Only then will you begin to feel the connection. Consider a few simple steps that you can begin doing to build this area:

1. Find something that you want to be involved in.
2. Be a good learner. Ask lots of questions and seek out someone who you see has some skills or ability that you would like to develop.
3. Show genuine interest in those with whom you interact. I know that this seems silly, but many veterans do not know how to make friends outside of the military.
4. Ask good questions about others and their lives. Assume that some aspect about them will interest you and be worth your understanding. *Tip: Be prepared to adjust your humor; non-military types don't always "get" our dark humor or off-color wit.*
5. Find a mentor and be willing to ask them to mentor you in the area(s) where you want to grow.

Get Spiritual

At the risk of sounding like a preacher, I need to return to this area. A growing body of research shows that service members and veterans who practice some faith expression display greater levels of resilience and have a significantly less troublesome transition than those who do not. I don't mean that those with faith expressions do not struggle with the transition, but I do mean that their struggles are notably less severe than those service members who lack a faith practice.

One research article published in 2014 tracked veterans who more easily made the transition into a civilian environment. That research identified several factors that made the transition either easier or more difficult. The chart below shows that the study did not look for anything distinctly "spiritual." It simply identified those who had an easier time of transition and those who had a more difficult time. I recommend that you spend a little time reflecting on this summary of the research and ponder its findings.

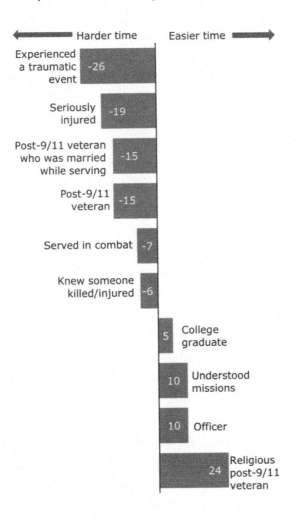

Notes: For percentages based on full sample of veterans, n=1,842; for post-9/11 veterans, n=710. Unless otherwise noted, subsequent charts are based on all veterans.

PEW RESEARCH CENTER

Notice that experiencing a traumatic event is typically one of the largest deficits to overcome; trauma makes the transition more difficult. On the opposite side of the spectrum, the factor that best improved one's chances to make a successful transition is religious activity.

The study highlighted that to gain this benefit, the veteran's spiritual practice had to be "robust," defined as being involved in some faith practice multiple times each week. Faith practice became a highly positive factor when veterans entered into it wholeheartedly. The study noted that having a robust faith practice was nearly equivalent in power (on the positive side) as suffering a traumatic service event (on the negative side). In other words, robust spiritual practice is a powerful factor in helping veterans to make a successful transition.

I hope you're asking, "Why should this be such a positive factor?" Remember that the critical issues creating transition difficulties include loss of meaning and purpose, identity confusion, and culture shock/loss. So, the question really should be, "How does a robust faith practice positively affect these areas"?

Most faith expressions and worldviews identify some form of purpose and meaning to living on this planet. This purpose and meaning are usually bigger than one's given vocation. Most faith expressions claim that a specific meaning and purpose for human life transcends everyday things. Consider Rick Warren's best-selling book, *A Purpose-Driven Life*. It proclaims a clear message that every one of us can live out a greater purpose that also has eternal significance. Warriors, too, can find a great purpose for their lives through faith, after they finish serving their country.

How do faith practices affect a person's identity? Since identity is grounded in a value system, and faith practices typically have strong value systems made clear through religious expression, personal identity cannot help but be influenced through a strong faith practice. Some faiths go into great detail about a person's given identity at a base level. Do you remember how one of the pillars of identity has to do with existential/spiritual influences? If a faith practice tells you that part of your identity comes from being "a child of God," a clear sense of identity goes with that description. But the most important way that faith influences identity—and how this makes a veteran's transition easier—is that it gives individuals an active identity that transcends one's military service.

Finally, let's ask how practicing faith lessens culture shock. One thing that makes culture shock so difficult is that many veterans feel as if they can find no like-mindedness with individuals in the civilian culture. Warriors fundamentally shifted their views of the world through their military experiences and training, and their "warrior viewpoint" often does not match the civilian viewpoint. A robust faith practice creates a belief system that transcends both military and civilian culture, fostering like-mindedness among adherents. It also typically creates some points of cultural agreement with the civilian community. These points of agreement help veterans to begin to relate with a community/culture in the civilian world, giving them areas where they can relate with others who may have no military background.

Don't give me wrong! I do not believe that you will agree with every area of some faith expression, especially when you have such a different life experience than most civilians. When you have a unified belief with a community, however, you can begin to create another tribe around you.

The power of a practiced faith creates a bridge back into the civilian world. You can find purpose and meaning that is bigger than your vocation and you can find an identity that is greater than "what you do." And you can find a culture to relate to around areas of shared belief. I make no claim that simply having a faith practice will easily fix all problems with the transition; but it is a powerful influencer that can greatly ease some of the difficulties.

On a very practical level, I began to notice this positive influence as I worked with many older veterans. I started to see that those who had a strong faith practice seemed to be less affected by their psychological injuries from Vietnam, even though those traumas were real and very powerful. Their faith seemed to create some factor that prevented the trauma from dominating their lives.

I use the metaphor of a wound. Even though they had wounds that deeply affected them, the wound never became infected. Many times, veterans that had the same wound, but without the antibiotic (faith practice), the wound became infected. And when the infection took over, it affected the whole body.

I do not mean that those without a faith practice are weaker, while those who have a faith practice are stronger. It has nothing to do with strength or weakness. It is simply a fact that individuals with a robust faith practice appear to be better able to interpret their experiences through a grid of greater purpose and meaning in a way that allows them to cope more effectively with their hardships and limitations.

One former force reconnaissance Marine with multiple combat deployments described to me his perspective on the impact of his faith practice: "Faith is what helped me find my way again. I struggled and floundered for multiple years; it was my faith that ultimately gave me an identity and purpose again."

This warrior eventually set up a nonprofit that took veterans and civilians to help people in need living in dangerous cultures. He took one team of veterans to Nigeria where they helped refugees flee from the Boco Haram. After his return, he told me about his experience: "I've had combat deployments and been connected with a brotherhood. It was just as profound and bonding to go to these places and help people in need with fellow veterans. And now I was doing it for an even greater purpose. There's no question the bond I got with these men was just as tight as men I went to combat with."

You can see how his faith practice not only helped him with his personal identity and purpose, but it also helped him bond and find deep camaraderie again.

Please don't think I am prescribing faith to anyone. I merely want to point out that current research says faith plays a major role in easing the transition. If you're reading this book, either you or someone you love is trying to get ahead of that transition or is attempting to address some struggles encountered during that transition. If you have no faith practice, it might be time for you to begin to look into it. If you do have a faith practice, it likely will be deeply meaningful for you to incorporate into your life at least some of its influences. I encourage you to lean on your faith practice and your faith community as you make this transition back into the civilian world.

A Warning

If you're about to get out of the military, let me give you a very important warning. You likely will apply for disability compensation through the department of Veterans Affairs, and rightly so. You should apply, because you no doubt have suffered some injuries in the service of your country, even if you were never deployed to combat.

There is, however, an even greater injury that can take place after you get out. Many active-duty warriors go from being strong performers on effective teams, to lone rangers who struggle with their transition, depending only on their disability compensation. The unfortunate result? They begin to take on a victim mentality.

A victim mentality is toxic because it puts a ceiling on your performance, your goals, and your aspirations for the future. If you take on the victim mentality, the best of what you've done with your life will be behind you.

Certainly, you deserve disability compensation for our injuries. But don't make it the primary focus of your future! Too many veterans take on a broken mentality because they are being paid for their disabilities, they need the money, they're struggling in the transition, and they allow a deep individual mentality to set in. This path only exaggerates the loss of identity and purpose. When a warrior goes from a place of strength to a personal identity that says, "I'm broken," the results can only be negative.

Understand, I'm *not* saying that if you get disability compensation, you take on a broken mindset. Warriors can be compensated for their injuries and not be victims. But to avoid the victim mentality, you need to continually press forward in a purpose for something bigger than yourself, even if it means losing some disability benefits.

I have often said that one of the worst things I see happening to warriors in transition is to get 100 percent disability. Even though it was given out of compassion, it can become a destructive force that negatively impacts the warrior for decades to come.

As warriors we need a purpose, and we need to be able to drive toward that purpose. Becoming a victim is the opposite of what a warrior is and the psychological consequence of this internal dissonance will only lead to a life of disappointment and despair.

A Final Word

This only a start. What I have provided is definitely not a "fix all." Remember, it took thousands of hours of intentional conditioning to make you into an effective war fighter. You will not undo it all simply by reading a book.

You will make the transition successfully only when you intentionally work to adapt to become a warrior citizen, rather than an active-duty warrior. When you do make the transition, however, you bring tremendous value back into the culture from which you came. If you don't adapt, you will lose much of the value of your military experience, or you will merely leave it in the past.

I urge you, *please* don't let this happen! Now, more than ever, our culture needs the immense value that warriors bring from their experience of life. The youth of this culture struggles tremendously with both identity and purpose, and when you successfully make the transition, you have great lessons available to be transferred to our youth.

I repeat now what I stated at the book's beginning: Not everything I have written will apply to you. But whatever does apply, seek to use it in your life. I cannot know every veteran's experience of re-entering the civilian world, but I have seen enough transitions (both healthy and unhealthy) to identify several key issues that are both common and prominent. If you see how this information applies to you, and you want it to have a potent, positive impact on the rest of your life, then let me repeat some advice I once heard about how to use a book to powerfully enhance your personal experience.

After you read the book the first time, go back and highlight the areas that you would like to return to for review. As you make those highlights, emphasize the things that you believe are especially important to you for personal application.

As you read through the book for a second time, review the notes you highlighted in each chapter. Ponder and carefully think over the concepts, rather than just reading them once and moving on. Contemplation and earnest pondering force our brain to hold onto the idea.

After your detailed review, read the book again; but this time; read it straight through without making highlights or stopping to ponder. Now you are trying to get the greater essence of the book as a whole and solidifying its primary concepts in your brain.

Frankly, it feels weird to give you this advice on reading my own book; but I would give the same advice about reading *any* book that you truly want to impact you.

Finally, and most critically: Don't accept the idea that you are broken. Even if you are injured, refuse to be broken.

You are a warrior. Now, bring that warrior mindset and adapt it to your new environment.

You are *not* broken. You are what you were made to be. The time has come to become what both you and your family need you to be.

ENDNOTES

‐‐‐‐‐‐‐‐‐ ★ ★ ★ ‐‐‐‐‐‐‐‐‐

i   Kenneth Conner, et al. "Post traumatic stress disorder and suicide in 5.9 million individuals receiving care in the veterans' health administration health system." *Journal of Affective Disorders*, 166 (2014) 1-5.

ii   Office of Suicide Prevention, *Suicide Among Veterans and Other Americans 2001-2014*, Department of Veteran Affairs (2016).

iii Smedly D. Butler, 1936.

iv M. Kuypers, USN.

v   Joseph A Vandello and Jennifer K Bossom, University of Florida. "Hard one and easily lost: review and synthesis of theory and research on precarious manhood." *Psychology of Men and Masculinity*, 2013, volume 14, No. 2, 101–113.

vi Dan Clay USMC, KIA 2006.

vii "Sacrifice," meaning 3, in *The Random House College Dictionary*, Revised Edition (New York: Random House, 1988), 1160.

viii Dominick Lucyk, CKOM News, "Humboldt Broncos crash survivors get together in first reunion since tragedy," July 26, 2021. https://panow.com/2021/07/26/humboldt-broncos-crash-survivors-get-to-gether-in-first-reunion-since-tragedy/

ix Gutman, Jack. *One veteran' journey to heal the wounds of war* (2016)

x   David S. Shepard and Frederic E. Rabinowitz, "The Power of shame in men who are depressed: Implications to the counselors." *Journal of Counselling and Development*, 451 (2013) Volume 91.

xi   Hadley C. Osran et al. "Living outside the wire: Toward a Transpersonal Resilience Approach for OIF/OEF Veterans Transitioning Back into Civilian Life." *The Journal of Transpersonal Psychology*, 2010, Vol 42, No. 2.

xii J. B. Stockdale, *Thoughts of a Philosophical Fighter Pilot* (Stanford, CA: Hoover Institution, 1995), 1998.

xiii Southwick, S., Charney, D. Resilience: *The Science of Mastering Life's Greatest Challenges* (New York: Cambridge University Press, 2018).

xiv M. Haller, PhD, Abigail C. Angkaw, PhD, Brittany A Hendricks, BA, and Sonya B, Norman, PhD. "Does reintegration stress contribute to suicidal ideation among returning veterans seeking PTSD treatment?". Suicide and life-threatening behavior 42 (2) April 2016.

xv   Southwick, S., Charney, D. Resilience: *The Science of Mastering Life's Greatest Challenges* (New York: Cambridge University Press, 2018).

xvi Southwick, S., Charney, D. Resilience: *The Science of Mastering Life's Greatest Challenges* (New York: Cambridge University Press, 2018).

xvii *The Difficult Transition from Military to Civilian Life.* (2014) Rich Morin. The Pew Social Trends.org: http://www.pewresearch.org/wp-content/uploads/sites/3/2011/12/The-Difficult-Transition-from-Military-to-Civilian-Life.pdf